To Denise

From mom w/Love

Cooking Up Country

Enjoy!

William Turner

COOKING UP

Country

A Collection of Recipes
Prepared for Country Music's
Top Stars on the Road

William L. Turner

BRANSON PUBLISHING COMPANY

1997

Branson, Missouri • Tucker, Georgia

Branson Publishing Company
P.O. Box 1232
Tucker, GA 30085

Manuscripts dealing with country music are solicited.
Materials will not be returned unless sufficient postage is enclosed in the package.

Photography:	Shirley Stanley
Project management:	Book Production Resources, Athens, GA
	www.bookproduction.com
Project co-ordinator:	C. Fred Thompson
Cover and text design:	Gore Studio, Inc., Nashville, TN
Pre-press production:	G&S Typesetters, Inc., Austin, TX
Printing and binding:	Data Reproductions, Inc., Auburn, MI

Library of Congress Cataloging-in-Publication Data

Turner, William L.
    Cooking Up Country / by William L. Turner

    Includes index.
    ISBN 0-9640690-1-6
    1. Recipes

To the ladies and gentlemen
who graciously shared their most
treasured recipes with me.

Contents

Weights, Measures, & Abbreviations

WEIGHT

1 ounce	=	approximately 28 grams
16 ounces	=	1 pound
1 pound	=	454 grams
1 kilogram	=	1,000 grams or 2.2 pounds
1 gram	=	1,000 milligrams

VOLUME

1 liter	=	1.06 quarts
1 gallon	=	3.79 liters
1 quart	=	0.95 liter
1 cup	=	8 fluid ounces
1 tablespoon	=	15 milliliters
3 teaspoons	=	1 tablespoon
16 tablespoons	=	1 cup

ABBREVIATIONS AND SYMBOLS

tsp.	=	teaspoon
tbsp.	=	tablespoon
lb.	=	pound
oz.	=	ounce
pt.	=	pint
qt.	=	quart
gal.	=	gallon
pkg.	=	package
F	=	degrees Fahrenheit
@	=	at
lg.	=	large
med.	=	medium
sm.	=	small

Preface

T HERE WAS a time, not so long ago, when many Southern families hurried to get the work done and the supper dishes washed before they gathered around the radio for their weekly Saturday night rituals. The dials were set and the static-chopped volume turned up a bit as Nashville radio station WSM crackled on the air with the Grand Ole Opry.

That radio set was as close as most folks ever got to the likes of Roy Acuff, Hank Williams, and Minnie Pearl. For those Saturday nights, at least, Nashville was Hollywood and Broadway, and the Opry was really the queen.

About the only thing that could pull a country music listener away from the radio on a Saturday night were those rare occasions when some big-name in the business stopped off at the local gymnasium for a show. The seats were hard, conditions cramped, and if the sound system produced an audible sound at all the show was a smashing success.

Unless one lived in a large city or could afford the pilgrimage to Nashville, there was no need to think about concerts and live shows. It was WSM on a Saturday night or nothing at all.

Nowadays, the stars of the Opry are passing each other regularly on roads all around the world. Draw a circle with a 50-mile radius anywhere on the map, and you can plot appearances during the year by a list of country music celebrities that reads like a Who's Who in the industry.

Live entertainment has followed right behind the rapid growth of the music industry throughout the world. As a result, the world has become the stage for country music entertainers. Today entertainers often travel to venues in

luxury buses and private jets. Crews and stage equipment commonly fill several eighteen-wheelers. For example, Reba's wardrobe fills an entire semi—one of a fleet of twenty-four. This is in stark contrast to the early days when several entertainers would travel together in the same automobile. It was not unusual for entertainers to travel with five or six adults per car with instruments tied to top of the vehicle. When bad weather occurred, space for the instruments had to be made inside the already cramped car. Because of the great distance between venues, many early entertainers drove all night to get to their next shows. Then, to save money, they set up camp on the outskirts of town rather than checking into a motel.

With today's spectacular stage productions, frequently it is necessary for the elaborate equipment to arrive several days prior to the show date. According to Pee Wee King, many of his early show were staged in rural school houses heated with pot-bellied stoves. The people who came to the show brought oil lamps from home and placed them in front of the entertainer—thus creating stage lights. The length of the show was often determined by the amount of oil in the lamps. The show was over when the oil was gone.

Pee Wee King fondly remembers his days of sharing vehicles with the likes of Gene Autry and Minnie Pearl. Before the era of the big time public relations firms, Minnie Pearl knew the importance of promotions. According to King, "Miss Minnie" spent the long car rides between shows answering fan mail and sending postcards to loyal fans announcing her appearances in their area. These gestures garnered her a loyal following and firmly established her as a major star.

Occasionally, local ladies served homemade desserts after the show. This act of kindness proved to be a smashing success and a real treat for the entertainers. While traveling, many entertainers' staple diet consisted of peanut butter and crackers, vienna sausage, sardines, and pork and beans. Many years passed before entertainers started to include

riders in their contracts that specified the meals to be served to them and their crew at the venue. The early contracts stated that the promoters supply a meal for the entertainer. The menu was determined by the promoters, who in turn, prevailed upon their wives to prepare the food. Wishing to impress the stars, the ladies prepared their "Sunday best" recipes. Many times they used fresh vegetables from the family garden. Some entertainers became so comfortable with this arrangement that they began to request their favorite dishes.

As the entourage grew in number, the promoter's wife had to seek help from her friends to prepare the meals. Not only was the entertainment business growing and changing but housewives were fast becoming caterers. One of the "perks" of being a caterer was getting to go backstage and meet the stars of country music. Even though the food may not now be prepared in the family kitchen, the same "Sunday best" recipes are still in use today. To meet the tastes of the entertainers, caterers are happy to prepare menus specified in the entertainer's contract.

Because of health reasons or personal preferences, a few entertainers choose to provide meals for themselves apart from the catered meals provided at the venue. For example, George Jones' wife, Nancy, prepares food for the two of them on their bus. Ty England will always choose his in-laws' home-cooked turkey and dressing over catered food.

One of the "perks" of being a journalist covering country music shows is having access to the backstage area. Not only did I meet and interview the stars of the stage but I also met and talked with the stars of the backstage—the caterers. Many of these caterers were happy to share their treasured recipes with me, and now I am happy to share them with you in *Cooking Up Country.*

EDITOR'S NOTE

Many of the recipes prepared by the caterers came from
personal family collections. These recipes may be increased by any
multiple in order to get the desired number of servings. The backstage
serving schedules vary greatly. The serving lines often begin with sound check
in mid-afternoon and continue until after the last show. Therefore, the
majority of the dishes must be good served at room temperature.
Meat dishes with mayonnaise in them should not be left out
more than an hour or so after first serving hot or cold.

Part One

APPETIZERS

FROSTED NUTS

1 egg white
1 tbsp. cold water
½ tsp. salt
½ tsp. cinnamon
¼ tsp. allspice
¼ tsp. cloves
½ cup sugar
2 cups nuts

- Preheat oven to 275 degrees. Combine egg white, water, salt and spices. Beat mixture until it forms a soft peak.
- Gradually add sugar, beating until mixture forms very stiff peaks. Add nuts a few at a time.
- Place on greased cookie sheet separated. Bake 40 to 45 minutes at 275 degrees.
- Store in tightly closed container.

Prepared for CMA post awards party.

"The Grand Ole Opry came on in 1925. Back then, the Grand Ole Opry had a lot of influence on the career of the artist. If you were not on the Grand Old Opry you could not get known nationally. And the Grand Ole Opry required you to be there every Saturday night."

—JOHNNY WRIGHT

FROSTED PECANS

1 lb. pecans (whole
    halves)
1 egg white
1 tsp. water
½ cup sugar
½ tsp. cinnamon
⅓ tsp. salt

- Beat egg white and water until frothy. Coat nuts with mixture.
- Mix sugar, cinnamon, and salt. Stir nuts in mixture until coated.
- Place nuts on buttered baking sheet and bake at 225 degrees for 45 minutes to 1 hour. Stir occasionally.

Prepared for Garth Brooks.

"**I** was late to the Grand Ole Opry only three times in fifty-three years. Judge Hay told me if I ever left the Grand Ole Opry I would have to fire myself."

—BILL MONROE

DIPPED STRAWBERRIES

1 qt. med. strawberries
12 oz. vanilla-flavored candy coating (for color variety add food coloring)

- Rinse strawberries and dry thoroughly. Set aside.
- Break candy coating into small pieces and place in a double boiler. Cook, stirring often, until coating melts.
- Dip strawberries into melted coating. Place on wax paper and let stand until coating hardens. For a festive look, arrange with strawberries dipped in powdered sugar.

Chocolate-flavored candy coating works equally well.

Prepared for James Bonamy.

"Judge Hay would turn over in his grave if he knew what was going on at the Grand Ole Opry today. He was of the old school—leave well enough alone."

—REDD STEWART

OVERNIGHT SHRIMP DIP

9 cups water
3 lb. medium shrimp
1 pkg. (8 oz.) cream cheese, softened
2 tbsp. fresh lemon juice
3 tbsp. salad dressing or mayonnaise
1 tsp. Worcestershire sauce
4 drops of hot sauce
½ tsp. salt
¼ tsp. pepper
⅓–½ cup minced green onion

- Bring water to a boil; add shrimp and return to boil. Reduce heat, and simmer 3 to 5 minutes. Drain well; rinse with cold water. Chill. Peel and devein shrimp; chop. Set aside.
- Combine cream cheese, lemon juice, salad dressing, Worcestershire sauce, hot sauce, salt and pepper; mix well. Stir in shrimp and onion; cover and chill 8 hours or overnight. Serve with assorted crackers.

YIELDS ABOUT 4 CUPS.

Prepared for CMA post awards party.

"If you really wanted to get to the old judge, all you had to do was to mention amplification. He wanted everything done in its original form, like Uncle Dave Macon, without amplifiers. Some places we went to play had coal oil lamps across the front of the auditorium. In those early days it was mostly school houses with big old pot bellied heaters in the back. People would bring lamps and set across the front as stage lights—no amplification at all."

—REDD STEWART

SHRIMP MOUSSE

2 lb. cooked and peeled
   shrimp
1 pkg. unflavored gelatin
¼ cup water
1 cup mayonnaise
1 cup sour cream
¼ cup diced green
   pepper
½ cup olives
¼ cup diced green onion
½ cup diced celery
2 tbsp. lemon juice
¼ tsp. hot sauce
1 tsp. dill
⅛ tsp. salt
1½ tsp. Worcestershire
   sauce
¾ tsp. paprika

- Combine gelatin and water in small pan; let stand 1 minute. Cook gelatin over low heat until gelatin dissolves, stirring constantly. Remove from heat.
- In food processor, combine gelatin, mayonnaise and remaining ingredients. In processor, mix 1 minute or until smooth. Add shrimp and mix well.
- Spray mold with vegetable cooking spray. Pour mixture into mold and press. Chill 8 hours or until firm. Makes 4½ cups. Put on tray and garnish with lettuce.

Prepared for a party for Vince Gill.

"**M**innie Pearl was one of the smartest people at the Grand Ole Opry in those days. She took all of the mail she got on Saturday and answered everyone the next week on post cards. She would write to all of these people and tell them where she would be appearing next. Just that personal thing kept all of us alive. The audiences today are in awe of the entertainers, but with us it was more of a family thing. We got to know the audience by their first names."

—PEE WEE KING

CHEESE BALL

2 pkgs. (8 oz.) cream
    cheese, softened
¼ cup bell pepper, diced
¼ cup onion, chopped fine
1 small can crushed
    pineapple (in its
    own juice), drained
2 cups chopped pecans

• Mix all together, mold and chill.

VARIATION:
Omit bell peppers and pecans. Form ball. Roll in
chopped pecans. Sprinkle with parsley flakes.

Prepared for Bryan White.

"**I** grew up singing with
my family and friends.
We sang at home and at
church. I never dreamed
that I would be in the
business like this when
I started."

—KITTY WELLS

BEEF AND CHEESE BALL

1 pkg. corned beef
4 green onions
¼ tsp. Ac´cent
1 tsp. Worcestershire
    sauce
1 pkg. (8 oz.) cream
    cheese

- Have cream cheese at room temperature.
- Chop beef and green onions. Mix all ingredients together. Shape in a ball.
- Chill several hours or overnight. Serve with Nachos or crackers.

Prepared for Tracy Byrd.

"In the early days, Kitty worked at a shirt factory and I worked at a furniture factory. We got up at 5 a.m. and did a thirty minute radio show and then went to work. Our co-workers would say that they heard us and that we did good. On weekends we played at school houses and if we made enough to buy gas and a hamburger we were happy. We loved it!"

—JOHNNY WRIGHT

CHEESE RINGS

1 lb. mild Cheddar cheese,
   grated
1 very small onion, grated
1 cup mayonnaise
1 cup chopped pecans
   red pepper to taste
   black pepper to taste

- Mix all ingredients and pour into jello mold. Refrigerate overnight.
- Serve with Smucker's strawberry preserves and Ritz crackers.

Prepared for Colin Raye.

"When I first started, women had to be careful or people would talk about them. Johnny and I got married in 1937 and we played schools and theaters around Nashville. I always traveled with Johnny. Times have changed and people don't think like they used to. They've gotten a little more liberal."

—KITTY WELLS

VEGETABLE DIP

1 pkg. (8 oz.) cream cheese
1 jar (13 oz.) marshmallow
　　creme
　milk (small amount)

• Blend cream cheese and marshmallow creme using milk to thin for desired consistency.

NOTE:
Powdered sugar may be substituted for marshmallow creme and lemon may be added for taste.

Prepared for Pam Tillis.

"The Prince Albert Network banned "Honky Tonk Angels" from their show. The original song said, . . . when I was a trustful wife . . . , meaning she could not be trusted. When I changed it to . . . trusting wife . . . they let me sing it."

—KITTY WELLS

ZESTY CHEESE SPREAD

2½ cups shredded sharp
    Cheddar cheese
    (10 ounces)
⅔ cup mayonnaise
2½ teaspoons lemon juice
1 teaspoon minced onion
2 tablespoons prepared
    mustard
2 teaspoons chopped
    pimento, drained
    dash of pepper

- Combine all ingredients, mixing well.
- Spoon mixture into a covered container; chill at least 1 hour or until ready to use.

YIELDS ABOUT 2 CUPS.

Prepared for George Strait.

> "**W**e traveled and entertained people just for the fun of it. There was little money to be made back then. We would charge 10 or 15 cents for our shows. We were singing for the fun of it."
>
> —JOHNNY WRIGHT

CHUNKY SANDWICH SPREAD

1 pkg. (8 oz.) cream
   cheese, softened
½ cup chopped onion
½ cup chopped green
   pepper
3 tbsp. chopped pimento,
   drained
3 tbsp. catsup
3 hard-cooked eggs,
   chopped
1 cup finely chopped
   pecans or walnuts
¼ teaspoon salt
¼ teaspoon pepper

- Combine all ingredients, mixing well.
- Spoon mixture into a covered container; chill at least 1 hour or until ready to use.

YIELDS ABOUT 3 CUPS.

Prepared for Garth Brooks.

"Our recording headquarters was in New York City. They would call and say that they would be at the Georgian Hotel in Atlanta, Georgia and for us to have four songs ready to record. The equipment was flown down from New York and placed in a room at the hotel. And we were placed in the room directly below the equipment. A light was dropped through the ceiling and when the red light came on we would sing. We had one mike for the singers and the fiddle player. We would step back to let the fiddle player get close. Another mike was there for the other musicians. We liked it better when we were all in the studio together."

—KITTY WELLS

Dijon Honey Dressing

1 cup mayonnaise
¼ cup Dijon mustard
¼ cup oil
¼ cup honey
⅛ tsp. onion salt
¾ tsp. cider vinegar
½ tsp. dried minced garlic
  pinch of red pepper

• Mix all ingredients well. Store in refrigerator.

Prepared for Suzy Bogguss.

"I've always been kind of shy. I feel that people who come out to see the show would rather hear me sing than to hear me talk—so I just sing. In the early days we didn't have people to lead and guide us. I just watched other performers. I just went out and acted like my self. It's always best to be yourself."

—Kitty Wells

PICANTE SAUCE

6 qt. tomatoes
4 cups bell peppers
4 cups chopped onions
¼ cup salt
½ cup sugar
2 tbsp. chopped garlic
½ cup chopped jalapeño
    peppers
2 cups vinegar

- Combine all the ingredients and boil slowly until thick. Be sure you don't scorch this as it thickens. Pour in clean jars and seal while hot.

Prepared for Leroy Parnell.

"**P**eople ask us when are we going to retire. I say, 'Why should we retire. We enjoy traveling—we are doing something we enjoy. The fans still buy our records and we still enjoy meeting the people.'"

—JOHNNY WRIGHT

VIDALIA ONION DIP

2	cups chopped onions
2	cups grated Swiss cheese
1½	cups light mayonnaise
1	cup seasoned bread crumbs
⅓	cup melted margarine

- Mix onions, cheese, and mayonnaise together in bowl.
- Mix margarine and bread crumbs together in separate bowl.
- Add half of bread mixture to onion mixture and mix well. Pour into a Pyrex baking dish and sprinkle remaining bread crumbs evenly over top. Bake at 350 degrees for 25 minutes. Serve warm with crackers or chips.

Prepared for Sammy Kershaw.

"**W**hen you are in country music, your fans follow you around all over the country. It's a lifetime commitment. And If you love it, you stay with it a long, long time."

—KITTY WELLS

SPINACH DIP

1 pkg. (10 oz.) frozen chopped spinach, thawed and drained
1 pt. Hellmann's mayonnaise
1 can chopped water chestnuts
1 medium onion, chopped
1 pkg. (2¼ oz.) vegetable soup mix
1 loaf French bread, sliced

- Mix the first 5 ingredients and let set for 1 hour before using. This will serve 20 people.

Prepared for CMA post awards party.

> "We started out traveling with two cars and a truck for the luggage and the instruments. Then we went to a stretch job and then to an airplane. Then we got a bus. Then we went back to two station wagons and a luggage truck."
>
> —PEE WEE KING

RAW VEGETABLE DIP

1 cup mayonnaise
2 beef bouillon cubes
⅓ cup boiling water
1 tsp. curry powder
½ tsp. garlic salt

• Dissolve beef bouillon cubes in the boiling water; mix all together.

Prepared for Terri Clark.

"**E**ddy Arnold, Uncle Dave Macon, Pee Wee and I were listening to the radio as we were riding to a job some place. Back in those days Eddy worshiped Bing Crosby. Uncle Dave Macon was sitting in the back seat and asked, 'Who is that singing, Eddard?' Eddy said, 'That's Bing Crosby, Uncle Dave.' Uncle Dave said, 'He'll never get anywhere singing songs like that.'"

—REDD STEWART

Part Two

SALADS

APPLE SALAD

2 large, crisp apples,
cut into med.
pieces
1 stalk celery, chopped
fine
¼ cup dates
¼ cup raisins
¼–½ cup walnuts
or pecans
⅛–¼ cup coconut
(optional)
1–2 tbsp. mayonnaise
1–2 tbsp. orange juice
(optional)

- Mix all ingredients together, making sure to coat apples evenly with mayonnaise. Refrigerate leftover salad.

Prepared for Ty England.

"Redd and I met J. L. Frank, Gene Autry's manager, and he hired us to play a show. After that, Red and I went to Knoxville and met Roy Acuff. Mr. Frank got us on The Grand Ole Opry."

—PEE WEE KING

FIVE CUP SALAD

1 cup mandarin oranges,
    drained
1 cup coconut
1 cup crushed pineapple,
    drained
1 cup sour cream
1 cup miniature
    marshmallows
  nuts (optional)

• Combine all ingredients. Chill at least 1 hour or overnight.

Prepared for Patty Loveless.

"We got the idea to write the Tennessee Waltz, thanks to Bill Monroe. Bill Monroe was from Kentucky and had written a Kentucky Waltz. The Tennessee Waltz is one of the greatest songs we ever composed together. Slow Poke was a million seller for RCA Victor. Back in our days, you had to sell a million records to get a gold record."

—REDD STEWART

COOL WHIP AMBROSIA

1 box (3.4 oz.) instant
  vanilla pudding
1 lg. (12 oz.) container
  Cool Whip
1 med. can chunk
  pineapple in heavy
  syrup
1 med. can mandarin
  oranges
1 med. jar maraschino
  cherries
1 med. can fruit cocktail
  in heavy syrup
1 cup miniature
  marshmallows
½ cup frozen coconut
½ cup chopped pecans

- Drain the pineapple, oranges, cherries, and fruit cocktail. Rinse and slice the cherries.
- Mix all together and leave in refrigerator until ready to serve.

Prepared for Jerry Clower.

"**R**edd, Shorty Boyd, and I were riding together from Texarkana to Nashville listening to the Grand Ole Opry and they were playing Bill Monroe's Kentucky Waltz. Redd pulled out a match box because we had used all of our paper. All we had was a big match box so we tore it open and wrote the Tennessee Waltz on it. Many times I wish we had kept that match box."

—PEE WEE KING

STRAWBERRY GELATIN SALAD

1 lg. pkg. strawberry jello
1 cup boiling water
1 sm. can crushed
    pineapple, well drained
1 pkg. (10 oz.) frozen
    strawberries

- Dissolve jello in boiling water. Add frozen strawberries and stir until thawed. Add ice water to make 1 quart. Mix in pineapple and pour into 1½ quart serving dish. Refrigerate until congealed.

TOPPING

1 pkg. (8 oz.) cream
    cheese
1 pkg. (8 oz.) sour cream
½ cup sugar
1 tsp. vanilla
1 cup chopped nuts

- Mix cream cheese and sour cream until smooth. Add sugar and vanilla. Spread over congealed fruit salad. Sprinkle chopped nuts evenly over top.

Prepared for Ronnie McDowell.

"The biggest change in our lives came when we moved from the Grand Ole Opry to do the television show. Mr. Craig thought TV was a passing fad. He said the Grand Ole Opry will never be televised. We went to Louisville with a one year contract and we've been there ever since."

—PEE WEE KING

BUTTERMILK SALAD

1 lg. can crushed pineapple
1 lg. Cool Whip
1 lg. pkg. peach jello
1 tsp. sugar
2 cups buttermilk
  chopped pecans

- In double boiler, add pineapple, jello and sugar; cook until dissolved. Cool slightly.
- Mix buttermilk and Cool Whip until blended. Add cooled mixture, pour in dish and chill.
- Garnish with pecans.

Prepared for Marty Raybon.

"The industry is too commercial today. In the early days all we thought about was survival—our attitude was to concentrate on entertaining the people. And we felt that the financial part would come. We got five dollars a day in those days. I would rather for the historians to say that we entertained the people than to say that we got rich."

—REDD STEWART

Pink Cloud

(Low Sugar)

24 oz. cottage cheese
20 oz. crushed pineapple
(unsweetened)
8 oz. Cool Whip
6 oz. sugar free
strawberry jello
¼ cup chopped pecans

- Drain pineapple. Stir cottage cheese and pineapple together. Add pecans, then stir in jello powder. Add Cool Whip. Mix well. Chill.

Prepared for Mark Collie.

"**W**e wanted to get acquainted with the people in the audience, so we would go out among them. Mr. Frank always told us to first sell your product, then you can go eat or whatever—always sell your product first. First, you get out there and meet those people, then you can go eat."

—Redd Stewart

CRANBERRY SALAD

1 lg. or 2 sm. boxes
   cherry jello
2 cans whole cranberry
   sauce
1 cup diced celery
1 orange, diced
2 med. apples, diced
1 can (15-½ oz.) crushed
   pineapple
1 cup chopped pecans

• Drain pineapple. Make jello with 2 cups boiling water; add 8 ice cubes and stir until melted. Partially gel while preparing remaining ingredients. Mix well and chill.

Prepared for Ty England.

"Country music is down to earth and tells a story of ordinary people. Pop music is created for stage shows and it really doesn't get down to earth."

—REDD STEWART

OLD-FASHIONED POTATO SALAD

2–3 lbs. potatoes
½ cup sliced green onions
⅔ cup thin sliced celery
6 hard-cooked eggs
1 tsp. salt
1 tsp. celery seed
¼ tsp. pepper
1 cup mayonnaise
1 tbsp. prepared mustard
½ cup sweet pickle relish
slices of pickles and hard-cooked eggs

- Boil, peel, and cube potatoes. Chop up 4 eggs, and slice 2 eggs and set aside.
- Combine potatoes, onions, celery, chopped eggs, salt, celery seed, and pepper in a large bowl.
- Blend mayonnaise, mustard and pickle relish. Gently stir into potato mixture and smooth top of mixture. Garnish with sliced pickles and eggs. Chill thoroughly before serving.

Prepared for Kitty Wells.

"**M**y mother-in-law made Gene Autry's first Palm Beach, off-white western suit. When he put it on he asked, 'Lydia, how do I look?' She said, 'Like a bundle of straw tied in the middle.'"

—PEE WEE KING

German Potato Salad

3 slices bacon
1 med. onion, chopped
1 tbsp. all-purpose flour
½ cup water
¼ cup cider vinegar
1 tbsp. sugar
1 tbsp. prepared
   mustard
½ tsp. salt
⅛ tsp. pepper
8–10 med. red potatoes
2 hard-cooked eggs,
   chopped
¼ cup chopped celery
2 tbsp. chopped
   fresh parsley

- Boil and peel potatoes. Slice enough to make 5 cups.
- Cook bacon in a large skillet until crisp; drain well, reserving drippings in skillet. Crumble bacon, and set aside.
- Sauté onion in bacon drippings until tender. Add flour, stirring until smooth. Gradually add water; cook over medium heat, stirring until thickened. Add next 5 ingredients; stir well, and bring to a boil. Stir in bacon and remaining ingredients. Serve immediately.

YIELDS 8 SERVINGS.

Prepared for Radney Foster.

> "I taught Pee Wee King how to wear a hat. I told him that you don't take a hat off like a chicken taking his comb off. You walk out there and bow as you take it off. Pee Wee would just walk out there and lift his hat up. I had to teach Pee Wee how to take his hat off."
>
> —GENE AUTRY

THREE BEAN SALAD

1 can green beans
1 can yellow wax beans
1 can red kidney beans
1 cup green pepper, finely
    chopped
¾ cup celery, finely
    chopped
2 med. white onions
½ cup vinegar
½ cup salad oil
½ cup sugar
1 tsp. salt

- Drain the beans. Cut medium-sized onions in half and thinly slice enough to make one cup.
- Combine vinegar, oil, sugar, and salt. Pour over beans, peppers, onions, and celery. Marinate overnight in refrigerator. Serve cold.

Prepared for Sonny Osborne.

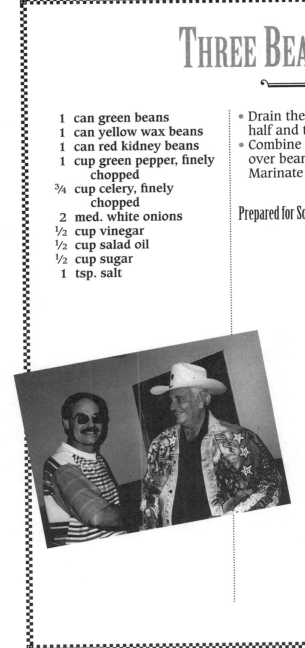

"**I** was mesmerized by Gene Autry. He didn't have to dance, blow out electric lights and smoke—he just went out on stage and started to sing *I'm Back In The Saddle Again.* The audience would just melt. People like Hank Williams and Ernest Tubb—I've seen audiences just go bananas and these guys didn't do anything but stand there and sing. Some of the big auditoriums did have spotlights. If you have the right kind of talent and can sing good enough, you don't have to do anything but sing."

—CHARLIE WALKER

BEAN SALAD

1 can French-style beans
1 can English peas
1 jar (2 oz.) pimento
1 cup celery, chopped
1 med. onion, chopped
½ cup vinegar
½ cup sugar
2 tbsp. cooking oil
¼ cup bean liquid

- Drain beans and peas, saving ¼ cup bean liquid.
- Arrange vegetables in covered dish. Place oil, vinegar, sugar, and bean liquid in boiler and bring to boil. Pour over vegetables. Let stand for 24 hours.

Prepared for Sammy Kershaw.

"To realize stardom you have to have a dream. When I was in the fifth grade, we were asked to write about what we wanted to be when we grew up. Most kids said a cowboy, a fireman, or whatever, but I wrote that I wanted to play on the Grand Ole Opry. I knew from that time what I wanted to do. You can't just sit and dream. You have to roll up your sleeves and work."

—CHARLIE WALKER

Sunshine Carrot Salad

2 cups carrots, grated
1 can (1 oz.) mandarin
    oranges, drained
1 cup pineapple chunks,
    drained
1 cup flaked coconut
½ cup raisins
1 carton (8 oz.)
    sour cream
    lettuce

• Combine first 5 ingredients; stir well. Chill 2 to 3 hours. Stir in sour cream; serve salad on lettuce leaves.

YIELDS 6–8 SERVINGS.

Prepared for Hal Ketchum.

"The only time I have been scared since I started in this business was when I did the Grand Ole Opry. I have never been so scared of going on stage. I think standing in the circle where so many greats have stood made me feel like all the ghosts of the former Opry stars were there with me.

—Sammy Kershaw

TOMATO ASPIC

1 pkg. (3 oz.) lemon jello
1 cup tomato juice
½ tsp. onion, grated
   juice of 1 lg. lemon
   dash of red pepper
1 cup cold tomato juice
¼ cup green stuffed olives,
   sliced
¼ cup celery, finely
   chopped

• In a saucepan, combine 1 cup tomato juice, onion, pepper, olives, and celery and simmer over medium heat for 10 minutes. Stir in gelatin until completely dissolved. Add cold tomato juice and fresh lemon juice. Congeal in mold until firm. Delicious served with cottage cheese.

Prepared for CMA post awards party.

"I grew up listening to the Grand Ole Opry. That's the kind of music I like."

—JOHN HARTFORD

TOMATO PETAL SALAD

6 med. tomatoes
1 cup peas
1 cup carrots, diced
1 cup celery, diced
1 tsp. onion, grated
¼ cup mayonnaise or salad
    dressing
1 tsp. sugar
1 tsp. lemon juice
    salt and pepper to taste
    lettuce leaves

- Use fresh or frozen peas and carrots. Cook and set aside.
- Scald and peel tomatoes; remove core. Cut a slice off the bottom; scoop out seed cavities. Refrigerate until ready to use.
- Combine remaining ingredients except lettuce. Cut tomatoes in six places almost to the bottom; spread the petals. Arrange on lettuce leaves; fill with pea and carrot mixture.

YIELDS 6 SERVINGS.

Prepared for Minnie Pearl.

"**B**eing inducted into the Grand Ole Opry and being the only member of the Grand Ole Opry that doesn't pick or sing is one of the most outstanding events in my career."

—JERRY CLOWER

SEAFOOD SALAD

1–1¼ cups cooked shrimp,
  crab meat or lob-
  ster (use only one
  or combine all 3)
 1 cup celery, thinly
  sliced
 ⅓ cup mayonnaise or
  salad dressing
 1 tbsp. green onion,
  minced
 ¼ tsp. salt
  dash of pepper

• Combine seafood and celery in bowl. Mix mayonnaise, onion, salt, and pepper. Pour over seafood and toss. Cover and chill at least 2 hours.

YIELDS 3–4.

NOTE:
For every 1 cup cleaned cooked shrimp needed, prepare ¾ pound fresh or frozen raw shrimp (in shells) or prepare 1 (7-oz.) package frozen peeled shrimp or use 1 (4½- or 5-oz.) can shrimp.

Prepared for Mercury Records awards party.

"**I** knew a lot of the Grand Ole Opry members before I moved to Nashville. They would come down to San Antonio and I would interview them for my radio show. Ernest Tubb, Stonewall Jackson, Jack Greene, Tex Ritter, and Red Foley helped me a lot when I got to Nashville. Mr. Acuff was nice to me and always invited me to come by and talk to him after the show."

—CHARLIE WALKER

EVERLASTING COLESLAW

1 head cabbage, chopped
1 onion, chopped
1 green pepper, chopped
1 carrot, shredded
1 tsp. salt
1 tsp. celery seed
1 tbsp. mustard seed
1 cup sugar
1 cup vinegar

- Mix together cabbage, onion, pepper, and carrot. Boil together remaining ingredients. Pour over coleslaw and refrigerate. This keeps for a month in the refrigerator.

Prepared for Daryle Singletary.

"**A** lot of the Louvin Brothers gospel music was like a sermon. I've seen people in the audience break out shouting."

—CHARLIE LOUVIN

Bob's Freezer Salad

1	cup white vinegar
1	cup water
¾	cup sugar
½	tsp. celery seeds
4	cups cauliflower flowerets
4	cups broccoli flowerets
1	lg. carrot, shredded
½	cup green pepper, chopped
½	cup sweet red pepper, chopped
1	med. onion, chopped
1	tsp. salt

- Combine first 4 ingredients in a saucepan; bring to a boil, stirring occasionally. Boil one minute. Cool.
- Combine broccoli and remaining ingredients in a bowl. Add vinegar mixture; toss. Pack into freezer containers, filling to ½ inch from top. Cover and freeze (up to one month).
- To serve, thaw in refrigerator 6 to 8 hours.

Prepared for Ken Mellons.

"I hope people will remember not what I've done but what I was—what I believed in. Your word is your bond. If your word is no good, people are afraid of your signature, too. First and foremost, a man should be true to himself."

—Charlie Louvin

Good Slaw

1	lg. head cabbage
1	tbsp. salt
1	mango
3–4	long pieces celery
2	cups sugar
1	cup vinegar
½	cup water
1	tsp. mustard seed

- Shred cabbage. Add salt and let stand 1 hour.
- Finely chop the mango and pieces of celery. Now squeeze the cabbage between hands into balls, like snowballs. Add mango and celery.
- Mix sugar, vinegar, water, and mustard seed. Simmer for 15 minutes. Pour while warm over cabbage and mix well. Refrigerate or keep cool overnight.

Prepared for George Strait.

"I have never to this day forgot where I came from. I spend time with the people. I've been criticized for being too accessible."
—Charlie Louvin

Zesty Slaw

1 lg. cabbage, finely shredded
1 lg. onion, chopped
1 lg. green pepper, chopped
1 cup pimento-stuffed olives, chopped
1 cup vinegar
1 cup olive oil
½ cup dill pickle relish
1 tsp. sugar
1 tsp. celery seed
1 tsp. garlic salt
½ tsp. salt
1 tsp. pepper

• Combine all ingredients in a large bowl; stir well. Cover and chill 1 hour before serving.

YIELDS 12 SERVINGS.

Prepared for Charley Pride.

"**M**ost of the time, in the early days, we traveled with the band in one vehicle—a station wagon. We once had an old gas powered bus but it gave us a lot of trouble. Regardless of the vehicle, traveling is therapy for me. I love it."

—CHARLIE LOUVIN

COLESLAW

4 cups cabbage, shredded
1 cup carrots, finely grated
¼ cup mayonnaise or salad dressing
2 tsp. lemon juice
2 tbsp. sugar
1 tbsp. evaporated milk
green pepper rings

- Combine first 6 ingredients; mix well. Cover and chill thoroughly. Garnish with green pepper rings.

YIELDS 4–5 SERVINGS.

Prepared for Garth Brooks.

"Country music is a fascinating business to be in. It is a wonderful career to have. However, you sacrifice a lot by being in this business. There's nothing normal about it—you're always away from home. You pop in once or twice in the spring and once or twice in the fall. But, all in all, it's very rewarding. Once you get started, it gets in your blood— you just know you're going to do this until you die."

—JANIE FRICKE

CARROT SLAW

2 cups carrots, shredded
1 cup cabbage, shredded
½ cup celery, thinly sliced
2 tbsp. onion, chopped
¼ cup corn oil
2 tbsp. cider vinegar
1 tsp. sugar
½ tsp. caraway seeds
⅛ tsp. pepper

• Mix together all ingredients in a bowl. Cover and chill.

YIELDS 4 CUPS.

Prepared for Ronna Reeves.

"**E**veryone who is an artist, who is a songwriter, will tell you that you don't have the time that you used to have before you started touring."

—JOE DIFFIE

MACARONI SALAD

1 pkg. macaroni and
   cheese dinner
1 can (12 oz.) Spam,*
   cut in chunks
½ cup celery, diced
½ cup carrots, shredded
¼ cup bell pepper, chopped
¼ cup sweet pickles,
   chopped
3 tbsp. onion, chopped
¼ cup salad dressing
¼ cup French dressing

- Prepare dinner as directed on package. Add remaining ingredients, mix lightly and chill.

Can substitute ½ lb. bologna.

Prepared for Rex Allen, Jr.

"It's a hard life to travel and then go home and everybody at the house is going to bed at 10:30 and you're used to staying up till 1:00 in the morning and sleeping till noon. So you have to adjust."

—REBA MCENTIRE

CONFETTI MACARONI SALAD

1 pkg. (8 oz.) or 2 cups
  elbow macaroni
1 can (12 oz.) luncheon
  meat, diced
1½ cups diced Cheddar
  cheese (6 ounces)
½ cup green pepper,
  chopped
⅓ cup onion, chopped
½ cup mayonnaise
2 tbsp. milk
2 tbsp. vinegar
½ tsp. salt
  lettuce

- Cook macaroni according to package directions; drain well. Combine macaroni, luncheon meat, cheese, green pepper, and onion; stir well, and chill.
- Combine mayonnaise, milk, vinegar, and salt; pour over macaroni salad, and toss well. Serve salad in a lettuce-lined bowl.

YIELDS 10–12 SERVINGS.

Prepared for Mel McDaniel.

"**I** know how to read a road map and I know how to sleep very well on the bus. I was always sleeping in a pickup or a car going down the road and I adjust very well to different time zones."

—REBA MCENTIRE

BROCCOLI SALAD

1 lg. head fresh broccoli, chopped
½ cup salted sunflower seeds
½ cup raisins
8 strips bacon, cooked and crumbled
½ cup onion, chopped
½ cup mayonnaise
½ cup sugar
1 tbsp. vinegar

• Combine broccoli, sunflower seeds, raisins, bacon, and onions in a large bowl. Mix together remaining ingredients and toss with broccoli mixture. Chill until serving time.

Prepared for Suzy Bogguss.

"For about five years, I traveled in a van with seven or eight guys, pulling a trailer, and stayed in bottom-of-the-line hotels. Now it's a breeze. I can go out to the bus and sleep after a show and arrive rested at the next gig."

—TRACE ATKINS

COLD BROCCOLI SALAD

1 head broccoli
1 bunch green onions, chopped
10 strips cooked bacon, cut up
1 cup Cheddar cheese, shredded

• Cut broccoli in small pieces. Combine with chopped onions, bacon, and cheese.

DRESSING

½ cup mayonnaise
1 tbsp. cider vinegar
¼ cup sugar

• Add dressing to the other ingredients.

Prepared for CMA post awards party.

"**W**hen something happens on the road, it needs to stay there. When you are done with the show, you need to get to bed and get some rest because there's going to be another show tomorrow in another town. I got into this business to have a little fun. The good Lord has taken care of us. He is driving the bus; that's all I can say."

—SAMMY KERSHAW

CAULIFLOWER SALAD

1 head cauliflower, cut in bite-size pieces	• Mix cauliflower, lettuce, and mushrooms. Let stand at room temperature for 30–60 minutes. Toss with dressing. Garnish with bacon.
1 head lettuce, chopped	
½–¾ lb. bacon, fried crisp and crumbled	
sliced mushrooms (fresh or canned)	

DRESSING

2 cups mayonnaise	• Mix sugar and cheese until smooth. Add mayonnaise and parsley flakes. Stir until well blended.
¼ cup sugar	
½ cup Parmesan cheese	
2 tbsp. parsley flakes (fresh, if available)	

Prepared for CMA post awards party.

"**T**hey did not have awards in the early days of my career. The first award I ever got was for the song *Will The Circle Be Unbroken* which I recorded with the Nitty Gritty Dirt Band. I had recorded that same song thirty years ago by myself."

—ROY ACUFF

CAULIFLOWER SALAD

1 cup mayonnaise
1 cup sour cream
1 pkg. cheese Italian salad
    dressing (dry mix)
    or onion soup mix
1 lg. head cauliflower,
    broken into sm. pods
1 cup radishes, sliced very
    thin
1 sm. onion, sliced
1 cup summer squash,
    sliced
1 cup cucumbers, diced
    or sliced
1 bunch (3 lg. stalks)
    broccoli, cut in flowers
    or pods

- Mix first 3 ingredients together and store in covered container in the refrigerator.
- Wash and drain vegetables. Mix together in a large bowl. Pour the dressing over the vegetables and cover with a lid. Store in a cool place for at least 2 hours. May be made the night before and stored in the refrigerator. When ready to serve, mix well and serve.

Prepared for the Oak Ridge Boys.

" I firmly believe that western music is the only true form of American music."

—REX ALLEN JR.

Hot Chicken Salad

4 cups cooked chicken, diced
1½ cups celery, finely chopped
1 cup toasted slivered almonds
1 tsp. salt
4 tbsp. onion, grated
1 cup green pepper, chopped
1 cup mayonnaise
4 tbsp. pimento, chopped
4 tbsp. lemon juice
1 can (10¾ oz.) cream of chicken soup, undiluted
2 hard-boiled eggs, chopped
2 cups New York State cheese, grated
crushed potato chips for topping

- Combine all ingredients except potato chips and cheese; blend well together. Spoon into a lightly greased 3-quart shallow casserole. Top with 2 cups cheese.
- Bake at 350 degrees for 30 minutes. Put sprinkling of crushed potato chips over surface during last 10 minutes.

YIELDS 8 SERVINGS.

Prepared for Minnie Pearl reception.

"I don't know who started country and western music. But to me, western music is like American folk music from the western part of the United States."

—Marty Robbins

CHICKEN SALAD

3–4 chicken breasts
    celery
    black pepper and salt
    garlic powder
    scallions (green
      onions)
    mustard
    mayonnaise

- Boil chicken with 1 or 2 sticks of celery, black pepper, garlic powder, or whatever seasonings you prefer. Cook until the chicken falls off the bone (should be very tender).
- Strip chicken; add mayonnaise sparingly. Add just a little mustard and chopped up scallions; mix well.

Prepared for Hall Of Fame Party.

"In my opinion, my greatest contribution to country music is the influence that I used to convince Decca Record executives to stop referring to our music as hillbilly music and to start referring to it as country and western music."

—ERNEST TUBB

SPAM AND MACARONI SALAD

1 can Spam, diced
3 cups elbow macaroni
1 cup sour cream
1 cup mayonnaise
¼ cup milk
½ cup sweet pickle relish
2 tbsp. vinegar
2 tsp. prepared mustard
¾ tsp. salt
2 cups cubed Cheddar
    cheese
1 cup celery, chopped
½ cup green pepper,
    chopped
¼ cup onion, chopped

- Cook macaroni according to package directions. Drain and rinse with cold water, set aside.
- Combine sour cream, mayonnaise, and milk, stir in pickle relish, vinegar, mustard, and salt.
- Toss together cooled macaroni, cheese, celery, green pepper, onion, and diced spam. Pour sour cream mixture over all; toss lightly to mix. Chill several hours or overnight. Spam may be browned and cooled if desired.

Prepared for Junior Samples.

"**I** originated Bluegrass music for all the world. Bluegrass and country music have different kinds of songs. In country music they don't keep the time like we do in bluegrass. Country music is a different kind of sound altogether."

—BILL MONROE

CURRIED CHICKEN SALAD

1 lg. orange
1 med. banana
4 cups torn mixed salad
 greens
2 cups chicken, cooked
 and cubed
 (12 ounces)
½ can (8 oz.) jellied
 cranberry sauce,
 chilled and cut in
 ½-inch cubes
¼ cup light raisins
¼ cup salted peanuts
½ cup mayonnaise
½ carton (4 oz.) orange
 yogurt
½–1 tsp. curry powder

- Section orange over bowl to catch juice. Slice banana diagonally and dip in reserved orange juice.
- Place salad greens in large salad bowl. Arrange orange sections, banana, chicken, cranberry cubes, raisins, and peanuts atop salad greens. Chill.
- To make dressing, combine mayonnaise, yogurt, and curry powder; chill. Serve dressing with salad.

Prepared for Janie Fricke.

"**B**luegrass is the music that's an outgrowth of the coming together of the music styles of Bill Monroe, Lester Flatt, Earl Scruggs, and Chubby Wise. Folk music is an outgrowth of the Pete Seegers movement and the older music style of American music. Country music is the movement of the outpouring of the Grand Ole Opry and western swing music. Bluegrass is a part of country music."

—JOHN HARTFORD

PORK AND BEAN SALAD

1 can (16 oz.) pork and
   beans
1 onion, chopped
3 tbsp. pickles, diced
4 boiled eggs, diced
   mayonnaise to taste

• Combine first four ingredients. Add mayonnaise to taste.

Prepared for Grandpa Jones.

> "**B**luegrass has a lot of gospel music in it—just enough to help the music along. There's a little blues in bluegrass and also a little Scotch-Irish influence."
>
> —BILL MONROE

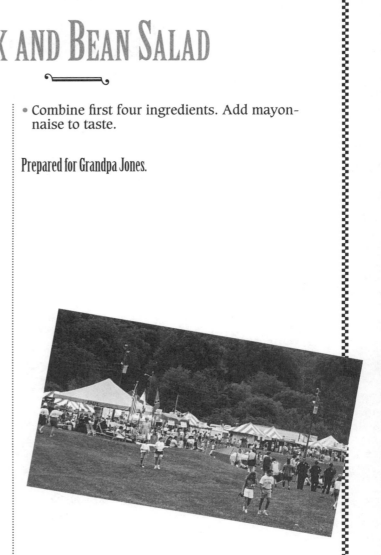

7 Layer Salad

2 cups lettuce, shredded
1 cup onion, diced
1 cup celery, diced
1 cup cauliflower, chopped
1 cup mayonnaise
1 cup crumbled bacon
1 cup grated cheese
1 can English peas

- Layer lettuce, onion, celery, cauliflower, and English peas.
- Spread mayonnaise on top and sprinkle with layer of bacon and layer of cheese. Refrigerate overnight. Toss salad prior to serving.

Prepared for Patty Lovelace.

"The first quality that comes to mind when I think of bluegrass is urgency. That's why it makes perfect sense to me that you often have very sad or even tragic lyrics in bluegrass being sung at what might seem like lively tempos. When I hear a song like that, I hear the music being pushed forward, driven on by the forcefulness of whatever it is they're singing about. To me that's the elusive quality that separates 'bluegrass' from 'close to bluegrass.'"

—GREG EARNEST

English Pea Salad

1 can (14½ oz.) French-
cut green beans
1 can (14½ oz.)
English peas
1 jar (2 oz.) pimentos
1 cup celery, chopped
2 med. onions, chopped
1 cup vinegar
¼ cup sugar
¼ cup Wesson oil
½ tsp. paprika
2 tbsp. water

- After draining, mix beans, peas, and pimentos with celery and onions.
- Heat vinegar, sugar, Wesson oil, paprika, and water, stirring until paprika and sugar are dissolved. Pour over vegetables. Chill overnight in refrigerator.

Prepared for The Gatlins.

"**B**luegrass is an important music—like jazz. Bluegrass is the last art form of basic music. All age groups like bluegrass. Songs that were popular in the thirties are still popular today. Some songs are so good that it's hard to do a bad version of that song."

—Mac Wiseman

MARINATED VEGETABLE SALAD

1 can (14½ oz.) French
  or cut green beans
1 can (14½ oz.)
  English peas
1 med. onion, chopped
2 cup celery, chopped
1 bell pepper, chopped
¼ cup pimento, chopped
1 cup vinegar
1½ cup sugar
½ cup Italian dressing
  salt and pepper to taste

- Drain beans and peas, saving ½ cup English pea juice. Add juice to vinegar.
- Simmer beans and peas in ½ cup pea juice until tender. Drain and combine with other ingredients. Refrigerate overnight.

Prepared for CMA post awards party.

"**B**luegrass has been a profound influence on country music. You almost have an acceptance of bluegrass artists in the country music field. Scaggs brought country music back from Vegas to Nashville."

—DOUG FLOWERS

Guacamole-Filled Avocado Halves

2 lg. avocados, halved
juice of 1 lemon
½ cup onions, finely
chopped
¼ tomato, chopped
½ tsp. salt
2 tbsp. cilantro, minced
tortilla chips
salsa

- Scoop the avocado from the shells—leaving about ⅛-inch rim. Squeeze the lemon juice over the empty avocado shells and the pulp.
- Mash the avocado pulp and combine with the remaining ingredients to make the guacamole filling. Return the filling to the shells. Surround with chips and salsa to garnish.

Prepared for Mercury Records party.

"Here we were—these long haired kids from California—we turned a lot of people on to blue-grass."

—Jeff Hannah

EASY DEVILED EGGS

6 eggs, hard-cooked
¼ cup mayonnaise
1 tbsp. sweet pickle relish
1 tsp. vinegar
½ tsp. Worcestershire
    sauce
¼ tsp. salt
¼ tsp. dry mustard
    paprika

- Slice eggs in half lengthwise, and carefully remove yolks. Mash yolks with mayonnaise. Add remaining ingredients, except paprika. Stir well.
- Stuff egg whites with yolk mixture. Garnish eggs with paprika.

YIELDS 6–8 SERVINGS.

Prepared for Loretta Lynn.

" **A** song is like a diamond. The diamond looks different when it's put in a different setting. A pop song can become a bluegrass song if it is put in a bluegrass setting."

—MAC WISEMAN

Part Three

MEATS

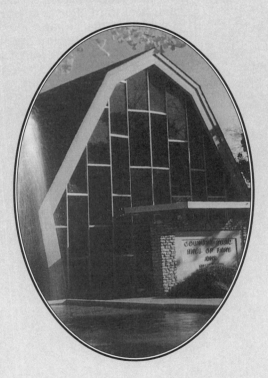

OLD FASHIONED FRIED CHICKEN

"The Stanley Brothers, the Flatt and the Scruggs and the Monroe sounds were first. We need to keep the old sounds alive. You can do your own style but keep the original sound."

—BOBBY OSBORNE

- Soak 1 fresh chicken in salt water for at least 30 minutes. Dry off and dip in buttermilk. Dredge chicken in flour that has been seasoned with salt, pepper, and paprika. Pour oil about 2 inches deep into an electric skillet, and heat until almost smoking. (To make it really good, use 3 parts cooking oil and 1 part bacon grease.) Be sure the oil is deep enough and hot enough. Brown chicken on both sides, turn the temperature down, place the lid on and cook covered 5 minutes on each side. Take the top off, raise the temperature to crisp the chicken, then cook for 15 to 20 minutes more. Total cooking time is 25 to 30 minutes.

- To make gravy, discard all but a small amount of grease in electric skillet. Take 2 tablespoons flour and mix with about ½ cup water. Pour this into skillet with drippings and brown. Slowly add room temperature milk and stir until thickened. Season with salt and pepper. Recipe works well for buffalo wings.

Prepared for CMA post awards party.

CHICKEN BREASTS IN SOUR CREAM WITH MUSHROOMS

8 slices dried beef
8 pieces (halves) boneless chicken breasts
8 half strips bacon
1 carton (8 oz.) sour cream
1 can (10¾ oz.) cream of mushroom soup

- In 9×13 inch Pyrex dish, arrange dried beef slices on bottom. Put one piece of chicken breast on each slice of beef and top with the half strip of bacon.
- Bake at 325 degrees for 45 minutes. Remove from oven and do not drain bacon grease.
- Mix together sour cream and soup. About 15 minutes before serving, pour mixture over meat. Return to oven and bake at 400 degrees until bubbly and golden. Serve with rice and a green salad for a great buffet dish.

YIELDS 8 SERVINGS.

Prepared for Holly Dunn.

"**B**luegrass is played on acoustic instruments. Every band has a Martin guitar, a Gibson banjo, a Gibson mandolin, the best kind of fiddle you can find and an upright bass. The high tenor singing would go in there, too. That's bluegrass!"

—BOBBY OSBORNE

Chicken Ruby

6 chicken breasts
⅓ cup all-purpose flour
1 tsp. salt
4 tbsp. butter or
   margarine
1½ cups fresh cranberries
¾ cup sugar
¼ cup onion, chopped
1 tsp. grated orange peel
¾ cup orange juice
¼ tsp. cinnamon
¼ tsp. ground ginger

- Flour and salt chicken, and lightly brown in butter.
- Combine remaining ingredients in saucepan and bring to boil. Pour over chicken. Cover and cook slowly, 35 to 40 minutes or until tender. Serve with rice or mashed potatoes.

Prepared for Minnie Pearl.

"If you can play blue-grass, you can play just about anything. It's a good school of music. You learn to sing, you learn to sing harmonies and you also learn to keep time."
—Doug Flowers

CHICKEN SUPREME

4 boned chicken breasts
cardamon
chervil
salt and pepper
1 egg
¼ cup milk
fine bread crumbs
butter or margarine
2 oz. brandy
4 tbsp. Burgundy
1 pint chicken stock

- Season chicken breasts with cardamon, chervil, salt, and pepper.
- Beat egg and milk together. Dip chicken breast into egg mixture, then into bread crumbs. Brown chicken on both sides in butter until tender.
- Place chicken in baking dish large enough to hold it in one layer. Pour the following over chicken: brandy, Burgundy, and chicken stock. Bake at 350, until tender and done.

YIELDS 4 SERVINGS.

Prepared for T. G. Sheppard.

"**B**luegrass fans are different from country music fans. Bluegrass fans attend festivals and bring their instruments and gather in the parking lot and play together. They bring entire families and camp out and actually participate in the festival."

—BOBBY OSBORNE

DIXIE SPECIAL BARBECUE CHICKEN

1 broiler-fryer chicken, quartered
½ cup catsup
¼ cup Mazola corn oil
1 can (8 oz.) tomato sauce
2 tbsp. onions, finely chopped
2 tbsp. water
2 tbsp. brown sugar
1 tbsp. Worcestershire sauce
1 tbsp. lemon juice
1 tsp. Ac´cent flavor enhancer
1 tsp. salt
⅛ tsp. pepper

- Make sauce by mixing together all ingredients except chicken. Brush mixture on chicken.
- Place chicken on outdoor grill. Cook approximately one hour or until done, turning and brushing with sauce while cooking.

YIELDS 4 SERVINGS.

Prepared for Vern Gosdin.

"**R**adio stations were trying to compete with TV in the early days of TV. To attract the audience, radio stations went to rock, top forty, etc. Bluegrass had a hard time keeping up."

—MAC WISEMAN

HARVEST CHICKEN

2 broiler-fryer
chickens, halved
1½ tsp. Ac´cent flavor
enhancer
2 tsp. salt
½ cup Mazola corn oil
2 tbsp. grated orange
peel
1½ cups orange juice
2 tsp. instant minced
onion
½ tsp. ground ginger
¼ tsp. hot pepper sauce
4 tsp. corn starch
2 tbsp. water
½ cup slivered almonds,
toasted
2 oranges, sectioned and
divided
2 cups seedless grapes,
some in clusters
parsley

- Sprinkle chicken on both sides with flavor enhancer and salt. Heat corn oil in Dutch oven over medium heat. Add chicken, brown on both sides. Remove from pan. Repeat until all pieces are browned.
- Return chicken to skillet. Add orange peel and juice, onion, ginger, and pepper sauce. Cover; simmer 20 minutes or until done.
- Place chicken on heated platter; keep warm. Blend corn starch into water; stir into sauce in skillet. Cook, stirring constantly, until mixture thickens, comes to boil and boils 1 minute. Add almonds, ½ of the orange sections, and grapes—reserving grape clusters for garnish. Heat gently. Spoon a little sauce over chicken. Serve remaining sauce separately. Garnish with parsley, remaining orange sections, and grapes.

YIELDS 4 SERVINGS.

Prepared for Ricky Van Shelton.

"**B**luegrass music has survived and been kept alive because children are introduced to bluegrass at a very early age. They come to festivals with their parents and get in free. But at country music shows, everybody pays. It's sort of like Sunday school— you introduce children to it at an early age and it becomes a part of them."

—SONNY OSBORNE

HONEY CHICKEN

1 can (20 oz.) pineapple
   slices in juice
4 chicken breasts, boned
   skinless halves
2 tsp. vegetable oil
2 cloves garlic, pressed
1 tsp. thyme, crumbled
1 tbsp. cornstarch
¼ cup honey
¼ cup Dijon mustard

- Drain pineapple slices; reserve juice.
- Sprinkle chicken with salt and pepper to taste. Rub with garlic and thyme. Brown in hot oil in non-stick skillet.
- Combine 2 tablespoons reserved juice with cornstarch. Combine honey and mustard; stir into skillet with remaining juice. Spoon sauce over chicken. Cover and simmer 15 minutes.
- Stir cornstarch mixture into pan juices. Add pineapple. Cook; stir until sauce boils and thickens.

SERVES 4.

Prepared for Rona Reeves.

"I see myself as a bit of a bridge between the old-timers like Johnny Cash, Ernest Tubb, Lester Flatt, Roy Acuff, Bill Monroe, and today's generation. I feel like I'm the link between the old world of country music and the new world of country music."

—MARTY STUART

OVEN FRIED CHICKEN

1 broiler-fryer chicken,
    cut in serving pieces
¼ cup Mazola corn oil
¼ cup sour cream
1 tbsp. lemon juice
1 tsp. Worcestershire
    sauce
1 tsp. Ac´cent flavor
    enhancer
1 tsp. celery salt
½ tsp. paprika
1 cup soda cracker crumbs

• Mix together all ingredients except chicken and crumbs. Dip pieces of chicken into mixture; then roll in crumbs. Place in a single layer in shallow baking pan and bake at 350 degrees oven for approximately 1 hour or until done.

YIELDS 4 SERVINGS.

Prepared for Doug Stone.

"The younger kids are discovering or rediscovering country music. Country now has sex symbols and I think that has helped a lot. In the past, country was limited by its reputation of being twanging and stuff."

—JOE DIFFIE

ROLLED CHICKEN BREASTS

10 chicken breasts
   garlic salt to taste
10 sm. onion slices
10 slices Swiss cheese
10 slices dried chipped beef
   or shaved ham

- Flatten chicken breasts between waxed paper. Sprinkle with garlic salt. On each breast place a slice of onion, cheese, and beef or ham. Roll up and fasten with toothpicks.

SAUCE

1 carton (8 oz.) sour
   cream
1 can (10¾ oz.)
   mushroom soup
   juice of one lemon
¼ tsp. paprika

- Combine 4 sauce ingredients. Pour over chicken. Bake covered for 1½ hours at 300 degrees. Uncover and cook for 30 minutes more.

YIELDS 10 SERVINGS.

Prepared for Pam Tillis.

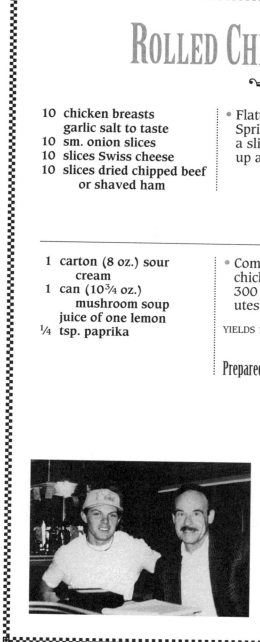

"I'm bridging the gap between the new generation of country music listeners and country music."

—DAVID KERSH

SKILLET CHICKEN AND RICE

3 tbsp. butter
⅔ cup rice, uncooked
1 can (4 oz.) mushroom
   stems and pieces
1 envelope (1½ oz.) dry
   onion soup mix
2 cups chicken, cooked
2 cups water

• Melt butter in electric skillet, and add rice and mushrooms with liquid. Stir in dry onion soup mix. Add chicken and water and mix. Turn skillet to low and cook covered about 30 minutes or until rice is tender.

YIELDS 6 SERVINGS.

Prepared for Joe Diffie.

"**I** feel that I'm a part of two generations. I grew up around the grand ladies of The Grand Ole Opry and other greats of country music. My mom was a great cook. She loved to cook. Our kitchen was always full of people. Kenny Rogers and Glenn Campbell were around our house a lot. The Gatlin Brothers even lived at our house for a while. And they were like a part of the family. These people are still bigger than life to me."

—SHELLY WEST

SKILLET STICKY CHICKEN

    2 tbsp. oil
2½–3 lb. chicken, cut up
    1 pkg. dehydrated
          onion soup mix
   ½ cup apricot or peach
          preserves
   ½ cup barbecue sauce
   ¼ cup water

- In skillet over medium heat, cook chicken pieces in hot oil until browned on all sides. Pour off fat.
- In small bowl, combine remaining ingredients. Stir into skillet. Reduce heat to low; cover and simmer 30 minutes until chicken is tender, stirring occasionally.

YIELDS 4 SERVINGS.

Prepared for Billy Dean.

"I think Kitty Wells, Loretta Lynn, Patsy Cline, and Tammy Wynette blazed the trails for the women of country today. Without people before you, you have no path to follow. I've always liked stylists even better than just singers because you recognize them when you hear their voices. I think uniqueness is a large part of longevity in country music."

—TERI CLARK

Sweet 'n' Smoky Oven Barbecued Chicken

1 broiler-fryer chicken,
   quartered
1 lg. onion, sliced
1 tsp. Ac'cent flavor
   enhancer
1 tsp. hickory smoked salt
¼ tsp. pepper

- Place chicken, skin side up, in shallow baking pan. Tuck onion slices in and around the chicken. Sprinkle Ac'cent, hickory smoked salt, and pepper on chicken. Bake, uncovered, at 370 degrees for 30 minutes.

BARBECUE SAUCE

½ cup catsup
½ cup Mazola corn oil
½ cup maple syrup
¼ cup vinegar
2 tbsp. prepared mustard

- Make barbecue sauce by mixing 5 ingredients together. Pour barbecue sauce over chicken, and bake 30 minutes longer or until done.

YIELDS 4 SERVINGS.

Prepared for Danny Shirley.

"Women like Jean Sheppard, Dottie West, and Patsy Cline were stylists. That's what makes an artist. You need to develop your own style. The stylists are the ones who have longevity."

—Gayle Strickland

SOUTHERN FRIED CHICKEN

1 fryer, cut into serving-
   size pieces
1 egg
   milk or buttermilk
   flour
   salt
   pepper
   cooking oil or solid
     shortening
   butter (optional)

- Salt fryer pieces, cover well, and refrigerate overnight.
- Beat egg and add milk or buttermilk. Dip salted fryer pieces in the mixture, making sure they are completely covered. Dredge in a mixture of flour, salt, and pepper. Place in a skillet filled with hot cooking oil and fry, uncovered over medium heat, until chicken is tender and golden brown on both sides. Make sure chicken is not crowded while frying. Drain well and serve.

NOTE:
The cooking oil (or shortening) should be very deep to properly fry the chicken. The addition of a small amount of butter to the oil adds special flavor and a golden brown color. Watch to be sure the butter does not burn.

Prepared for Bill Monroe.

"**P**eople in the music industry who have had longevity are those personalities that can and do relate to an audience."

—REBA McENTIRE

VEG-ALL CHICKEN POT PIE

1 chicken, stewed and
   deboned
2 cans cream of potato
   soup
1 can Veg-All, drained
½ cup milk
½ tsp. thyme
½ tsp. black pepper
2 frozen pie crusts
   (9-inch), thawed
1 egg, slightly beaten

• Cut up chicken into bite sized pieces. Combine first 6 ingredients. Spoon into prepared pie crust. Cover with top crust; crimp edges to seal. Slit top crust and brush with egg, if desired. Bake at 375 degrees for 40 minutes. Cool 10 minutes.

Prepared for Redd Stewart.

"You can go to church and find women who can sing and sound good, but to be a success their voices have to be different. That's what it takes to make a star."

—OWEN BRADLEY

Coq au Vin

½ lb. bacon, diced
2 tbsp. butter
2 fryers, quartered
16 whole mushrooms
16 sm. white onions
2 cloves garlic, crushed
3 tbsp. flour
1 tsp. salt
2 tbsp. chives, chopped
½ tsp. thyme (¼ tsp. if dried)
¼ cup parsley, chopped
⅛ tsp. pepper
2 cups Burgundy
1 cup chicken stock
16 sm. new potatoes

- In Dutch oven, sauté bacon until crisp. Remove. Add butter to drippings and brown chicken well. Remove. Add mushrooms and onions. Cook until nicely browned, then remove.
- Pour off all but three tablespoons fat. Add garlic. Sauté 2 minutes. Stir in flour, salt, chives, thyme, parsley, and pepper. Cook until flour is browned, about 3 minutes. Gradually stir in Burgundy and chicken stock. Bring to a boil, stirring. Remove from heat. Stir in bacon, chicken, onions, and mushrooms. Cover and refrigerate overnight.
- Next day add scrubbed new potatoes to the chicken mixture. Bake covered at 375 degrees about 2 hours or until chicken and potatoes are tender. Serve with noodles or brown rice.

YIELDS 8 SERVINGS.

Prepared for CMA post awards party.

"I schooled myself listening to Patsy Cline. I was always striving to achieve the emotion, volume, and control she used in portraying a song."

—REBA McENTIRE

BARBECUED FRANKS

1 tbsp. butter
½ cup onion, chopped
1 tsp. paprika
4 tsp. Worcestershire
   sauce
¼ tsp. Tabasco
¼ cup catsup
1 tsp. pepper
1 tsp. mustard
4 tsp. sugar
3 tbsp. vinegar
6 franks and buns
   fresh green onions

- Melt butter. Add onions and cook until clear. Add all seasonings, sugar, and vinegar.
- Cut a 3-inch slit in each frank and place in flat baking pan slit side up. Add sauce mixture. Bake in 350 degrees oven for 20 minutes. Baste frequently. Place franks in buns, garnish with fresh green onions. Serve extra sauce separately.

YIELDS 6 SERVINGS.

NOTE:
Franks can be cut in 1-inch pieces and served heated in sauce as appetizers.

Prepared for Janie Fricke.

"The biggest obstacle today is being a female entertainer. If it's hard today, I can only imagine what it was like when the grand ladies of the grand Old Opry began their careers. If they had not started back then and stayed with it, we could not be where we are today."

—RONNA REEVES

LITTLE SMOKIES

3 pkg. Smokies (sausages)
    by Oscar Mayer
1 bottle (12 oz.) Heinz chili
    sauce
1 jar (10 oz.) grape jelly

• Heat in crock pot and serve.

Prepared for CMA post awards party.

" **I** used to sit in Tootsies and get chill bumps just thinking about the people whose presence once graced the chairs, the stools, and the bar. And just think, I got to play there and be a little part of the history of country music."

—TERI CLARK

Mexicali Hot Dogs

vegetable cooking spray
8 frankfurters
1 can (8 oz.) tomato sauce
1 cup water
3/4 cup onion, chopped
1/2 cup green pepper, chopped
1 tbsp. brown sugar
2 tbsp. prepared mustard
2 tbsp. hot pepper, chopped
1 tsp. chili powder
1/2 tsp. salt
8 hot dog buns

- Spray a large skillet with vegetable cooking spray. Pierce frankfurters with a fork in several places, and cook in skillet until lightly browned.
- Combine next 9 ingredients in a large saucepan; bring to a boil. Add frankfurters; reduce heat, and simmer 10 minutes or until sauce is thickened. Serve in warm hot dog buns.

YIELDS 8 SERVINGS.

Prepared for Neal McCoy.

"**D**olly Parton is glamour to me. I've been a fan of hers for years. I got to meet her and sing with her on one of her albums. Even up close and personal, she is a glamorous, magnetic lady—very smart and very personable. She is really larger than life and that takes a unique gift. For me, the glamour is the fact that I can make a living in the music business and work with a lot of talented people."

—Lari White

FRIED STREAK O'LEAN

Sliced streak o'lean
Milk
Flour
Cooking oil

• Select the number of slices needed. Soak several hours in milk. Drain. Coat with flour. Fry over medium heat in small amount of oil until crisp. Be sure it is done. Drain on absorbent paper.

NOTE:
A Southern dish that is as good with vegetables as with breakfast food.

Prepared for Bill Monroe.

"**Y**ou may be out there, standing by the bus, hot and sweaty but you feel glamorous because of the way the fans treat you. They make you feel special. That's a real good feeling."

—SHELLY WEST

ROAST BEEF HASH

5–6 med. potatoes
1 med. onion
1 tbsp. cooking oil
½ tsp. garlic, minced
½ stick margarine
2 tbsp. dried parsley
flakes
1 can (12 oz.) Armour
Star roast beef
salt and pepper
to taste

- Pour cooking oil in bottom of black skillet or large frying pan. Cut potatoes into round slices. Cut onion into slivers; break up the roast beef over potatoes already layered in pan. Salt and pepper to taste and add parsley and garlic. Cut margarine into pats and cover all the mixture with water.
- Start cooking on high heat until ingredients come to a hard boil (this is done while pan is covered). Turn heat down to medium; uncover. When potatoes start to soften cut potatoes in small pieces. Stir occasionally. When water turns gravy-like and mixture is thick, hash is done.

SERVE AS 2 LARGE PLATES (MAIN MEAL) OR 4 SMALL HELPINGS.

Prepared for Pee Wee King.

"Country music has finally gone down all the different avenues. I don't think it's gone as far in each avenue as it's going to. There's now a contemporary market; there's a bluegrass market; there's a gospel market; there are all types of country music. It will continue to grow in all directions with a lot of new artists coming along. I think country music is definitely the music of today."

—T. G. SHEPPARD

SKILLET BEEF AND MACARONI

1 lb. ground beef
¼ cup onion, chopped
2 cans (8 oz.) tomato sauce
1 can (12 oz.) whole kernel corn
1 cup cooked macaroni
2 tsp. chili powder
½ tsp. seasoned salt
½ cup (2 oz.) Cheddar cheese, shredded

- Cook ground beef and onion in a skillet until browned; drain well.
- Drain the corn. Stir in next 5 ingredients. Simmer, stirring occasionally, 5 to 10 minutes or until thoroughly heated.
- Stir in Cheddar cheese.

YIELDS 4–6 SERVINGS.

Prepared for Johnny Wright.

"I feel that if God gives us a talent, we need to try to do with it what we can. If we do the right thing with it, He blesses what we do. I cannot take credit for anything. If I had not been blessed with a talent and other attributes He gave me, I would still be picking in beer joints."

—CHARLIE DANIELS

BEEF AND BEANS

1 lb. ground beef
1 onion
2 cans (16 oz.) baked
    beans
1/2 cup brown sugar
3 tbsp. margarine
    salt and pepper to taste
1/2 cup catsup
    dash of Worcestershire
    sauce
1 tsp. dry mustard

- Cook onion in margarine.
- Salt and pepper meat, add the onions and cook until crumbled.
- Put beans, brown sugar, catsup, Worcestershire, and mustard in Pyrex dish and mix with spoon. Cover beans with onion mixture. Bake 45 minutes for 1 hour at 350 degrees.

Prepared for Ken Mellons.

" **M**y music is not intended to get a message across— my music is meant to entertain people."
—CHARLIE DANIELS

MARINATED ROAST

15–17 lb. roast
1 cup sherry
½ cup wine vinegar
½ cup olive oil
8 cloves garlic, crushed
1 tsp. dry mustard
2 tsp. soy sauce
2 tsp. rosemary
2 tsp. salt

- Mix all ingredients and marinate the roast in the refrigerator for 10 to 24 hours, turning several times.
- Bake at 350 degrees for 30 minutes, then at 275 degrees for about 6 hours. Adjust baking time for rare or well-done roast.

SERVES 18–20.

NOTE:
Perfect for before or after concerts, or backstage parties.

Prepared for Terri Clark.

" **C** ountry music is just plain music—no frills. I see nothing wrong with coming out on stage and just singing your songs. I don't see what fireworks and stuff like that has to do with a country song."

—MARK CHESNUTT

GRILLED SALMON

4 salmon steaks or fillets
olive oil
1 green pepper, cut into
thin slices
12 black olives, pitted
1/2 cup sweet onion, finely
chopped
1 tsp. garlic, minced
1 1/2 cup tomatoes, chopped
1/4 tsp. oregano
1/4 tsp. red pepper flakes
1 bay leaf, crushed
salt and pepper

- Combine the green pepper, olives, onion, garlic, tomatoes, oregano, red pepper flakes, bay leaf, and salt and pepper in a bowl; stir. Set aside.
- Get the charcoal fire going and allow it to burn down to ashy gray coals. Place the grill about 6 inches above the coals. Place a 12-inch strip of heavy-duty aluminum foil on a flat surface. Lay 1 salmon steak in the center of the foil. Put 1 teaspoon olive oil and one quarter of the mixture on the steak. Fold the long sides of the foil over the fish, making an airtight fold along the entire length of the foil. Fold up the end of the foil, leaving some space inside to allow for expansion. Place the 4 foil packets on the grill and cook for about 15 to 18 minutes, depending upon the thickness of the steak.

Prepared for Grand Ole Opry birthday party.

"I think if you are in country music, you are a traditionalist whether you like it or not."

—RADNEY FOSTER

SIMPLE SLOPPY JOES

1 lb. ground beef
1 med. onion, chopped
½ cup catsup
3 tbsp. vinegar
2 tbsp. water
1 tbsp. brown sugar
1 tbsp. dry mustard
1 tbsp. Worcestershire
    sauce
¼ tsp. salt
    hamburger buns

- Cook meat and onion in a large skillet until meat is browned; drain off drippings. Stir in next 7 ingredients, and heat thoroughly. Serve in warm buns.

YIELDS 4–6 SERVINGS.

Prepared for Ken Mellons.

"I am proud to be involved in the tradition of country music and in the tradition of singer/songwriter that has been around Nashville for years. I have played on the Grand Ole Opry and that is a thrill that no one can ever take away from me."

—RADNEY FOSTER

SMOKEHOUSE HAM LOAF

3 tbsp. butter, melted
½ cup brown sugar
1 can (8 oz.) crushed
   pineapple
1 lb. lean ground ham
2 eggs, slightly beaten
1 cup quick oats
   (one minute)
½ cup milk
¼ tsp. pepper
¼ tsp. ginger
1 tbsp. prepared mustard

- In a 9×5 inch loaf pan, combine the butter and brown sugar. Drain the pineapple, reserving ¼ cup of the juice. Spread the pineapple over the butter and brown sugar.
- In a separate bowl, combine the reserved juice and the remaining ingredients and mix well. Press into the prepared pan. Bake in a 350 degree oven for 50 minutes. Invert the loaf to serve.

YIELDS 6 SERVINGS.

Prepared for Roy Acuff.

"**I** personally believe that if you are a traditional country artist, you will have longevity in this business because that's where it all started."

—KEN MELLONS

TENNESSEE HAM

1 ham
1 cup dark molasses
  whole cloves
1–1½ cups brown sugar
  meal or cracker
    crumbs
  fruit preserves

- Completely cover the ham in cold water; allow to soak overnight. Take out and remove any hard surface. Put in suitable pot with fresh water, skin side down; add molasses. Cook slowly allowing 25 minutes to the pound. Allow to cool in the liquid.
- Pull skin off carefully. Score ham. Stick a clove in each square. Sprinkle with paste made of brown sugar, crumbs, and sufficient liquid to make the paste. Bake slowly in moderate oven for 1 hour.
- Decorate the platter with thin ham slices cut from the roast ham. Roll slices into cornucopias and fill with fruit preserves.

Prepared for Grandpa Jones.

"I want to be just as hard core country as I can stand to be."

—TY ENGLAND

STUFFED GREEN PEPPERS

6 lg. green peppers
1 lb. ground beef
2 cups dry bread crumbs
   or cracker crumbs
2 tsp. salt
2 tbsp. onion, chopped
½ tsp. pepper
2 cans (16 oz.) tomato
   sauce

- Heat oven to 350 degrees.
- Cut thin slice from stem end of each pepper. Remove all seeds and membranes; wash inside and outside. Heat one cup water and 1 tsp. salt to boiling. Add peppers. Cook 5 minutes and drain.
- Mix remaining ingredients and lightly stuff each pepper with the meat mixture. Stand peppers upright in ungreased baking dish. Cover and bake for 45 minutes. Uncover and bake 15 minutes longer.

Prepared for Reba McEntire.

"The country music scene *is* the American culture. The country music scene has never been as popular as it is right now. I think that we have grown steadily. One of the things that really caught on was when Elvis Presley took country and rhythm and blues and combined them. That's the reason why I say that Presley opened the door for everybody and this is one of the driving forces of creating what the music scene is all about."

—MICKEY GILLEY

STUFFED PEPPERS WITH RICE AND HAM

6 lg. green peppers
1 sm. onion, chopped
¾ cup celery, chopped
2 tbsp. butter or
   margarine
2 med. tomatoes,
   chopped
2 cups cooked rice
1½ cups cooked ham,
   chopped
½ cup chopped
   almonds, toasted
½ tsp. salt
¼ tsp. pepper
½ cup buttered bread
   crumbs

- Cut off top of green peppers, and set aside; discard seeds. Cook peppers 5 minutes in boiling salted water; drain and set aside.
- Chop tops of peppers, combine with onion and celery, and sauté in butter in a large skillet until tender. Add next 6 ingredients. Cook 15 minutes or until most of liquid is absorbed.
- Stuff vegetable mixture into peppers, and top with buttered bread crumbs. Place in baking dish, and pour in 1 inch of water. Bake peppers at 350 degrees for 10 minutes.

YIELDS 6 SERVINGS.

Prepared for Marty Stuart.

"I make traditional country music—music that country people can relate to."

—DARYLE SINGLETARY

HAM DELIGHTS

½ lb. margarine
3 tbsp. mustard
3 tbsp. poppy seeds
1 med. onion, chopped
1 tbsp. Worcestershire
¾–1 lb. ham
⅓ cup Swiss cheese, cut in squares

- Blend first five ingredients together in a bowl.
- Split 3 dozen party rolls or Parker House rolls. Spread both sides with preceding mixture.
- Shred ham and cheese and place between rolls that have been spread with mixture. Wrap in foil and bake 20 minutes at 400 degrees.

Prepared for Ken Mellons.

" **M**y early heroes were guys who sang with feeling—Buck Owens, Lefty Frizzell, Keith Whitley, Vern Gosdin, John Anderson—guys who were performance driven as opposed to perfection driven."

—KEN MELLONS

HAM ROLLS

1 pkg. (3 oz.) cream
  cheese, softened
2 tbsp. green pepper,
  finely chopped
2 tbsp. pimento, chopped
  and well drained
1 tbsp. mayonnaise
1½ tsp. creole mustard
6 (6×4×⅛ inch) boiled
  ham slices

- Combine all ingredients, except ham. Spread cream cheese mixture evenly on one side of each ham slice; roll up and secure with a wooden pick. Cover and chill.
- Carefully slice each roll into ½ inch pieces; serve with toothpicks.

YIELDS 4 DOZEN.

Prepared for John Anderson.

"Conway Twitty was an awesome entertainer because he was so real. He was who he was. He did music nobody else did, but so did Marty Robbins. Hank Williams, Sr. has been dead for over thirty years but his music still lives. That's what keeps country music alive."

—GAYLE STRICKLAND

GLAZED MEATBALLS

1 lb. ground beef
¼ cup milk
¼ cup dry bread crumbs
¼ tsp. pepper
¾ cup onion, minced
1 egg
½ tsp. salt
¾ cup catsup
½ cup water
½ tsp. salt

- Combine the first seven ingredients. Shape into balls. Brown in small amount of fat.
- Combine catsup, water, and salt. Pour over meatballs and simmer 20 minutes, turning frequently.

Prepared for CMA post awards party.

"**G**eorge Strait is a country stylist who has not changed. He may put a little edge on his music sometimes but he's still traditional country."

—DARON NORWOOD

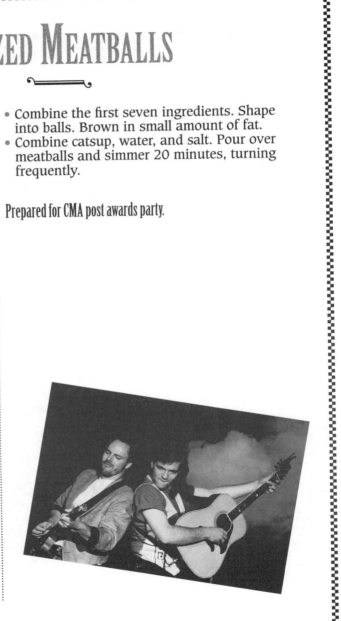

DOTTIE'S SWEDISH MEATBALLS

1½ lb. ground chuck
½ lb. lean ground pork
¼ cup milk
1 cup cooked rice
1 egg, beaten
1½ cup dry bread crumbs, finely chopped
¼ cup Crisco oil
1 tbsp. parsley
2 tsp. Morton Season-All
¼ tsp. marjoram
¼ tsp. basil
¼ tsp. black pepper
¼ tsp. thyme
1 tsp. garlic salt
1 lg. onion, finely chopped
¼ tsp. celery salt
½ cup bell pepper, finely chopped
1 can (10¾ oz.) cream of mushroom soup (Do not add soup when mixing, forming meatballs.)

- Mix meats together. Add and mix ingredients by kneading them one at a time into the meats. Makes about 24 large meatballs.
- Put in large Corning Ware dish sprayed with Pam. Cover with cream of mushroom soup that has been heated in saucepan. Cover, cook 350 degrees for 1 hour 15 minutes; 15 minutes before done pour almost all broth off.

Prepared for Dottie West.

"I feel that I'm helping to keep country music country. I couldn't care less about having a crossover record. I feel like I'm helping to keep the traditional sound in country music."

—GEORGE STRAIT

SWEDISH MEAT BALLS

2 tbsp. onion, minced
2 tsp. margarine
1 lb. ground chuck or round
½ cup quick rolled oats, uncooked
1 egg, slightly beaten
1 tsp. salt
⅛ tsp. pepper
¼ tsp. caraway seed
3 tbsp. margarine or more
1 can (10¾ oz.) cream of celery soup
½ cup water

- Brown the onion lightly in the margarine in a small pan over low heat.
- Combine the meat, oats, egg, seasonings, and cooked onion until thoroughly mixed. With floured hands, shape the meat into 45 small balls (1 inch in diameter). Fry them slowly in margarine in a heavy skillet until brown, turning on all sides. As browned, remove.
- When all are browned, add the soup and water to the skillet drippings and stir until smooth and bubbly. Return meat balls, cover tightly, simmer over low heat for 20 minutes or until done. Serve at once or cool, chill, and reheat later. They may also be frozen for later use.

YIELDS 6 SERVINGS.

Prepared for CMA post awards show.

"**I** found out about Bob Wills from George Strait, who is my biggest influence."

—DAVID KERSH

Pork Tenderloin

1 pork tenderloin
  (2½–3 lb.)
¼ cup soy sauce
¼ cup bourbon
2 tbsp. brown sugar

• Mix marinade of soy, bourbon, and brown sugar. Marinate in glass dish several hours in the refrigerator. Return to room temperature. Bake at 300 degrees for 2 hours, basting frequently. Slice and serve with cold sauce.

SAUCE

⅓ cup sour cream
⅓ cup mayonnaise
1 tbsp. dry mustard
1 tbsp. chopped green
  onions
1½ tsp. wine vinegar
  salt and pepper

• Blend and serve on the side.

YIELDS 4–6 SERVINGS.

Prepared for Mac Wiseman.

"The new listeners, the generation who is growing up with me listening to and supporting country music—it's real important for them to know about Bob Wills, George Jones, Buck Owens, and Merle Haggard. Even if it's through other artists, they are getting the history of traditional country music."

—David Kersh

SAUSAGE BALLS

2–3 cups Bisquick mix
8 oz. extra sharp
    shredded cheese
1 lb. hot sausage

- Mix cheese and sausage, then Bisquick mix. Roll into balls and bake at 350 degrees for 15 to 20 minutes, until brown.
- Can be frozen prior to baking; add 15 minutes to baking time. May roll and cut as cookies to bake.

Prepared for CMA post awards show.

"It's very flattering to be recognized as one of the guys who is continuing traditional country music. I grew up listening to country music. It's something I've got in my heart and I've got to let it out."

—DARYLE SINGLETARY

BEEF TENDERLOIN

1 beef tenderloin (4–6 lb.)
    dry mustard
    salt and pepper
    mild steak sauce
        (optional)
    mushrooms (optional)

- Trim tenderloin closely. Generously sprinkle with dry mustard and rub surface well. Salt and pepper to taste. Place in shallow roasting pan. Brush steak sauce over tenderloin. Roast in preheated oven at 450 degrees for 30 to 40 minutes (rare) or 45 to 60 minutes (medium) being careful not to over-bake.
- Slice 1 to 1½ inches thick or as desired. Serve hot. Serve plain or with mushrooms.

YIELDS 6–8 SERVINGS.

Prepared for Marty Raybon.

"**I** see myself just slightly left of center in traditional country music. I just love swing music and I believe that it's a part of musical history that doesn't need to go away. But today, it's just like pulling teeth to get a western swing song played on the radio."

—TRACY BYRD

Bea's Barbecue Beef Roast

4–5 lb. pot roast
  3 med. onions, chopped
  1 clove garlic, diced
  1 cup water
  1 can (8 oz.) tomato
     sauce
    salt and pepper
     to taste

- Brown roast on both sides.
- Add first 5 ingredients and cook at 325 degrees for 2 hours.

SAUCE

  2 tbsp. brown sugar
½ tsp. dry mustard
¼ cup lemon juice
½ cup vinegar
½ cup catsup

- Combine sauce ingredients. Pour over roast and cook an additional 2 hours at 325 degrees.

YIELDS 6 SERVINGS.

Prepared for Colin Raye.

"A lot of my style came from Haggard and listening to a lot of older guys when I was growing up."

—Trace Atkins

HAMBURGER STROGANOFF

1 lb. ground beef
½ cup onion, chopped
1 can (10¾ oz.) cream
    of chicken soup
1 can (8 oz.) mushrooms,
    drained
1 cup sour cream
2 tbsp. flour
¼ tsp. salt
¼ tsp. garlic salt
⅛ tsp. pepper

- Brown beef and onion in skillet over medium heat. Drain off excess grease. Stir in flour, salt, garlic salt, and pepper. Add undiluted cream of chicken soup and mushrooms. Let simmer 10–15 minutes.
- Stir in sour cream and heat thoroughly just before serving. Serve over hot noodles.

YIELDS 6–8 SERVINGS.

Prepared for CMA post awards party.

"**I**'m inclined to agree with the critics who say that there's not enough country music in country music right now. I need to hear more fiddles and steel guitars."

—KEN MELLONS

TUNA-MACARONI TREAT

1 pkg. (7¼ oz.) macaroni
   and cheese dinner
1 can (7 oz.) tuna, drained
   and flaked
1 can (10¾ oz.) cream of
   celery soup, undiluted
½ cup milk
1 tbsp. chopped onion

- Prepare macaroni and cheese dinner according to package directions, decreasing butter to 2 tablespoons, if desired.
- Drain and flake tuna. Combine remaining ingredients in a large bowl, and mix well; stir in macaroni and cheese. Spoon tuna mixture into a lightly greased 1½-quart baking dish. Bake at 350 degrees for 18 to 20 minutes until lightly browned.

YIELDS 4–6 SERVING.

Prepared for Minnie Pearl.

"I want country music to be the best music that it can possibly be. That's why I have such a passion for the history of country music and for what it stands for. We have to keep this alive."

—KEN MELLONS

SALMON BALL

1 can (1 lb.) salmon
1 pkg. (8 oz.) cream cheese, softened
1 tbsp. lemon juice
2 tsp. onion, finely chopped
1½ tsp. prepared horseradish
½ tsp. salt
½ tsp. black pepper
¼ tsp. Tabasco sauce
¼ cup pecans, chopped
3 tbsp. parsley, snipped

• Drain and flake salmon, removing skin and bones. Combine next 7 ingredients. Mix thoroughly. Chill several hours or overnight.
• Shape salmon mixture into ball. Roll in mixture of chopped pecans and parsley. Chill well. Serve with crackers.

Prepared for a Mercury Records party.

> **"I** think country music is one of the most flexible formats in radio. You can hear real hard country like Dwight Yokam or Randy Travis and it's great. You can hear a little more like rock or pop or Ricky Scaggs' bluegrass."
>
> —JEFF HANNAH

SHRIMP À LA CREOLE

4 lb. lake shrimp
4 green bell peppers
1½ cans Italian tomato paste
1 bunch shallots or 1 lg. onion
½ sm. pod garlic, sliced
¾ cup salad oil
3 heaping tbsp. flour
salt and pepper to taste (may add crushed pepper)

- Clean shrimp and boil for 5 minutes, then drain.
- Use iron skillet and make a roux with oil and flour; brown well. Add onions; brown slightly. Add salt, pepper, and shrimp. Stir around in roux until each shrimp is coated and none of the roux or onion sticks to the pan.
- Add tomato paste and green peppers and stir for 15 minutes on moderate heat. When paste begins to stick to shrimp, pour 1 cup hot water in skillet; cook on low heat. Let cook for 15 minutes more, then stir well and slowly add 3 to 4 cups hot water. If this method is used carefully, the rich gravy will cling to the shrimp. Cook for 1 hour before serving.

NOTE:
Famous New Orleans dish. If directions are followed carefully, this recipe can be successful.

Prepared for Sammy Kershaw.

"Country music speaks in very simple terms about a vast array of subjects, deep subjects, but in very simple terms that can be understood by both young and old."

—LIONEL CARTWRIGHT

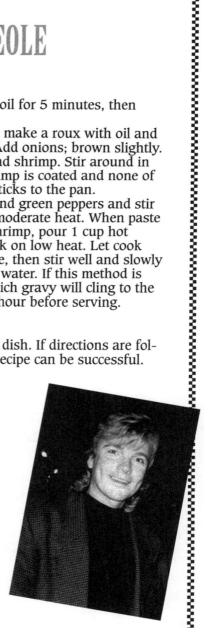

SHRIMP BALLS

4 pkg. (8 oz.) cream
cheese
3 cans tiny shrimp
3 tbsp. grated onion juice
1 tsp. lemon juice
½ tsp. Season-All
dash of paprika
dash of celery salt

- Cream cheese should be room temperature.
- Drain shrimp and mix with cream cheese.
- Combine all ingredients and chill overnight. Next day, roll in chopped nuts.

Prepared for Lee Greenwood.

"**I** think that the best thing country music has to offer is that you can tell stories. It tells real stories about real people. It is very reliable stuff, and it is really an American art form that caters to middle America."

—RADNEY FOSTER

"DIPPER'S NUGGETS" CHICKEN

6	whole broiler-fryer chicken breasts, skinned and boned
2	eggs, beaten
1	cup water
1	cup flour
3	tbsp. sesame seed
1½	tsp. salt
1	tsp. Accent flavor enhancer
1–1½	pints Mazola corn oil

- Cut breast pieces into 1×1½ inch nuggets. Mix eggs and water. Add flour, sesame seed, salt and flavor enhancer to make batter.
- Heat corn oil in fry pan over medium heat, with pan no more than ⅓ full. Dip nuggets into batter; drain off excess batter. Place nuggets in oil and fry about 3 to 5 minutes or until golden brown and done. Drain on paper towels. Serve with following sauces.

YIELDS 12 SERVINGS.

Nippy Pineapple Sauce:
In saucepan, mix 1 jar (12 oz.) pineapple preserves, ¼ cup prepared mustard and ¼ cup prepared horseradish. Heat.

YIELDS 1-1/2 CUPS.

Dill Sauce:
In bowl, mix ½ cup sour cream, ½ cup mayonnaise, 2 tablespoons finely chopped dill pickle, and 1 tsp. dried dill weed. Let stand at room temperature for 1 to 2 hours to blend flavors.

YIELDS ABOUT 3/4 CUP.

Royalty Sauce:
In saucepan, mix 1 cup catchup, ½ teaspoon dry mustard, 1 tablespoon brown sugar, 2 tablespoons vinegar, 6 tablespoons margarine. Mix and cook 4 to 5 minutes stirring constantly.

YIELDS 1 CUP.

Prepared for Radney Foster.

> "**I** think country music is a good forum in that it presents itself as a way to speak to people."
>
> —JEFF HANNAH

Part Four

CASSEROLES

GRANDPA'S BRUNSWICK STEW

2 broiler-fryer chickens, cut in parts
2 qt. water
2 lg. onions, sliced
2 cups okra, sliced
4 cups fresh tomatoes, chopped
2 cups lima beans
3 med. potatoes, diced
4 cups fresh corn, cut from cob
2 tsp. salt
1 tsp. ground black pepper
1 tbsp. sugar (optional)

- Simmer chicken in water in large saucepan, covered, at least 1 hour or until meat can be removed from bones. Cut chicken into bite-size pieces.
- Add vegetables to chicken broth and simmer, uncovered, until tender (30 minutes).
- Add salt, pepper, sugar, and chicken to vegetables mixing well and simmer about 15 minutes more. Check and stir occasionally to prevent scorching.

Prepared for Grandpa Jones.

"This business revolves around a song. I love country music, I love to hear those people who created this music. You don't get any better than Merle Haggard, Buck Owens, and Lefty Frizzell."

—RONNIE McDOWELL

WESTERN BRUNSWICK STEW

3 cups cooked chicken, chopped
1½ lb. coarsely ground chuck
½ lb. coarsely ground lean pork
1 lg. onion, chopped
1 lg. bottle catsup
2 (No. 3) cans tomatoes, mashed
2 (No. 3) cans yellow cream-style corn
1 dried red pepper
  or
1 tsp. ground red pepper

- Cook chicken and pull from bones.
- Cook together beef, pork, and onion in 1 cup of chicken stock with just enough water to cover meat. Cook slowly for 1 hour; salt to taste.
- Use scissors to cut up chicken. It's easier. Add catsup and tomatoes; cook another hour. Add corn, chicken, and red pepper. Cook slowly another hour and stir often (very easy to stick). This is 3 hours cooking time in all.

NOTE:
Use a heavy pot for cooking stew. Cook without lid after adding vegetables. A crock-pot may be used for cooking this stew if desired. It should be cooked down thick. If crock-pot is used, cooking time should be 8-10 hours.

YIELDS 15 SERVINGS.

Prepared for Chris LeDoux.

"As I get older I know what I really want to say, what's important for me to say, what God wants me to do—that's on my mind as an artist more than ever before."

—LEROY PARNELL

LITTLE-BITTY SAUSAGE QUICHE

½ lb. pork sausage, mild
2 eggs, beaten
½ cup milk
1½ tbsp. butter, melted
1 cup (4 oz.) Cheddar
cheese, shredded
pastry shells
paprika
parsley sprigs
(optional)

• Cook and drain the sausage. Combine first 5 ingredients; stir well and pour into prepared pastry shells. Sprinkle with paprika. Bake at 350 degrees for 20 to 25 minutes or until set. Garnish with parsley just before serving if desired.

PASTRY SHELLS

1¾ cup plus 2 tbsp.
all-purpose flour
1½ tsp. salt
4½ tbsp. butter, melted
1 egg yolk
5–6 tbsp. cold water

• Combine flour and salt; add butter, mixing well. Add egg yolk and water; stir with a fork until all dry ingredients are moistened.
• Shape dough into 36 (1-inch) balls. Place dough balls in lightly greased 1¾-inch muffin pans or assorted canape tins, shaping each into a shell. Prick bottom and sides of pastry shell with a fork; bake at 400 degrees for 5 minutes. Let cool on a rack.

YIELDS 3 DOZEN.

Prepared for CMA post awards party.

"I think that we need to be very careful about what we write because people hang on to every word we say."

—BOB DYLAN

AWARD WINNING CHICKEN CASSEROLE

3 cups chicken, cooked and diced
4 eggs, hard-cooked and chopped
2 cups rice, cooked
1½ cups celery, chopped
1 sm. onion, chopped
1 cup mayonnaise
2 can (10¾ oz.) mushroom soup
1 pkg. (3 oz.) slivered almonds
1 tsp. salt
2 tbsp. lemon juice
1 cup bread crumbs
2 tbsp. margarine, melted

- Combine all ingredients except bread crumbs and margarine, mixing well. Pour into one 3 quart oblong casserole, two 1½ quart casseroles, or three 1 quart casseroles.
- Combine melted margarine and bread crumbs and sprinkle over top. Bake at 350 degrees for 35 to 40 minutes or until bubbly and hot.

YIELD 12–15 SERVINGS.

Prepared for Patty Lovelace.

"**I** don't think that when Hank Williams, Sr., was writing songs he thought, 'I want to write it and I want it to sound right.' He was just writing out of his heart and that's what made him great. That's what makes all great songwriters and singers great; it's really coming from the heart."

—LIONEL CARTWRIGHT

Janie's Broccoli Chicken Casserole

1 pkg. (10 oz.) Birds Eye broccoli, chopped
1 cup Minute rice
1 cup chicken, cooked and diced
1 can (10¾ oz.) cream of chicken soup, condensed
1 cup milk
1 cup Cheddar cheese, grated
1 med. onion, chopped

- Place vegetable in 1½ quart baking dish. Bake at 350 degrees for 7 minutes to partially thaw.
- Stir in rice, chicken soup, chicken, milk, half of the cheese, and onion. Sprinkle with remaining cheese. Bake for 45 minutes or until hot and bubbly.

Prepared for Janie Fricke.

"'Leap of Faith' taught me not to be afraid to just write what's coming through me and through my spirit; just put it down and go with it. My best songs have just fallen out the sky. It's really weird—it's like you are not even thinking them up yourself."

—Lionel Cartwright

CHESTNUT CHICKEN CASSEROLE

3–4 chicken breasts,
    cooked and cut into
    bite-size pieces
2 cans (10¾ oz.) cream
    of chicken soup
1 sm. (8 oz.) sliced water
    chestnuts, drained
1 sm. onion, chopped
¾ cup almonds, sliced
1 cup celery, chopped
¾ cup mayonnaise
2 cups egg noodles,
    cooked
    potato chips

- Combine preceding ingredients and place in a 9×12 inch casserole. Bake at 350 degrees for 30 minutes. Top with crushed potato chips.

YIELDS 8 SERVINGS.

Prepared for Mark Chesnutt.

"**I** just try to listen to what my fellow man has to say. There are a lot of brilliant people out there in the heat of the battle of everyday living who are not songwriters, and would not know how to express themselves past the first line or little idea. But I try to listen to people, and to listen to my own conscience and the things I say. That's basically where I get inspiration."

—LARRY GATLIN

EASY CHICKEN CASSEROLE

1 whole chicken
1 carton (8 oz.) sour cream
1 can (10¾ oz.)
      mushroom soup
1 pkg. (1½ oz.) dry onion
      soup mix
1 can (3 oz.) chow mein
      noodles

- Cut chicken into serving pieces and place in a casserole large enough to hold chicken without crowding.
- Combine the sour cream, mushroom soup, and onion soup mix. Spread the soup mixture over the chicken. Cover with chow mein noodles and bake for 1½ hours at 325 degrees.

YIELDS 4–6 SERVINGS.

Prepared for John Anderson.

> **"I**'m like an old mare coming into heat. I know that about four or five times a year I'm going to sit down and whoop off some songs because I'm a songwriter."
>
> —LARRY GATLIN

Bar Ranch Chicken Casserole

3 lb. chicken, cooked and cubed
1 sm. pkg. corn tortilla chips, broken into sm. pieces
2 cups cheese, grated
1 can cream of chicken soup
1 sm. can tomatoes with green chili peppers
1⅓ cup chicken broth
1 stalk celery, chopped
1 med. clove garlic
1 cup onion, chopped

• Layer chicken, tortillas, and cheese in greased casserole dish; set aside.
• Combine soup, tomatoes, chicken broth, celery, garlic, and onion in saucepan; bring to a boil. Pour over chicken and bake at 325 degrees for 40 minutes.

Prepared for Danny Shirley.

"I write songs from the heart about things I've experienced in life or what some of my friends have experienced. I want my music to make people stop and think, 'Hey! I've been there.'"

—Gayle Strickland

CHICKEN RICE CASSEROLE

1 box (7 oz.) instant or quick rice, uncooked
1 can (10¾ oz.) cream of mushroom soup
1 can (10¾ oz.) cream of celery soup
½ cup milk
1 frying chicken, cut into pieces or preferred chicken parts
1 pkg. (1½ oz.) onion soup mix
1 can (4 oz.) mushrooms

- Grease a 9×13 inch casserole. Put rice in casserole.
- Mix the two soups and milk and heat until all are well blended (do not boil). Pour soup mixture over rice and stir slightly to moisten rice on bottom.
- Place chicken pieces on top of rice. Sprinkle chicken with onion soup mix, then with mushrooms. Cover with foil and bake at 325 degrees for 2 hours and 15 minutes.

Prepared for Lionel Cartwright.

"When I write a song, I can't make it too personal. Just because I understand it doesn't mean everyone else will. If I can write a song and everyone gets what I want them to get the first time they hear it, I've got a good song."

—TRACE ATKINS

Squash Casserole #1

2 lb. squash
1 stick margarine
1 onion, grated
1 carrot, grated
½ pt. sour cream
1 can (10¾ oz.) cream
    of chicken
    or
1 can (10¾ oz.) cream of
    mushroom soup
½ pkg. (4 oz.) seasoned
    bread crumbs
    (Pepperidge Farm)
    salt and pepper to taste

• Cut up squash and cook until tender. Drain thoroughly and add remaining ingredients. Sprinkle a few seasoned crumbs over the top. Put in oven and cook at 375 degrees until bubbly. Freezes well.

YIELDS 10–12 SERVINGS.

Prepared for Kitty Wells.

"**I** like to do songs that I can relate to. It is hard for me to be a dreamer. I get an idea for a song and I have it all written in my head—words and music—before I put it on paper. There are songs in my mind and in my heart that are ready to come out but I haven't taken the time to sit down and write."

—DARRELL McCALL

TEX-MEX SQUASH CASSEROLE

1	qt. squash, cooked
1½	cups soft bread crumbs
½	bell pepper, chopped
1	lg. onion
1	stick butter, melted
1	jar (2 oz.) pimentos
½	lb. cheese, grated
½	cup milk
½	cup celery, chopped
2	eggs, beaten

• Mix together all ingredients, saving out approximately one cup of the grated cheese. Place in buttered casserole dish. Sprinkle cheese on top. Bake at 350 degrees for 45 minutes.

Prepared for Neal McCoy.

> **"I** try not to write or make music that I would not listen to or that I would not want to own."
>
> —MARK COLLIE

Dottie's Squash Casserole

4 cups fresh squash,
  cooked
  or
2 cans (16 oz.) squash,
  drained
2 med. carrots, grated
1 med. onion, finely
  chopped
1 jar (2 oz.) pimento strips
1 can (10¾ oz.) cream
  of chicken soup
½ pint sour cream
1 stick margarine
1 pkg. Pepperidge Farm
  cornbread dressing
  mix

- Mash squash and mix with carrots, onions, pimentos, soup, and sour cream.
- In separate pan, melt the margarine and toss with dressing mix. Spread a thin layer of dressing mix in bottom of 9×13 inch casserole or two 8×8 inch casseroles.
- Alternate layers of squash mixture and dressing mixture. Finish with a thick layer of dressing mixture on top. Bake at 350 degrees for 30 minutes.

Prepared for Dottie West.

"I think that part of being a good songwriter is being observant with your own life and the lives of the people around you. If you write about those things, then you find something that appeals to a real broad audience, and yet, it can be very touching at the same time."

—RADNEY FOSTER

GENERAL JACKSON'S SQUASH CASSEROLE

2 cups squash, cooked
1 lg. onion, chopped med.
    to fine
1 cup sharp Cheddar
    cheese, shredded
2 eggs, well beaten
1 cup bread crumbs
    (Pepperidge Farm
    dressing mix)
1 cup milk
¼ tsp. garlic salt
    salt and pepper to taste

• Combine all ingredients and pour into greased casserole dish. Cover with aluminum foil and cook at 350 degrees for 30 minutes. Remove foil and turn oven up to about 500 degrees just long enough to brown the top.

Prepared for John Hartford.

"**I**'m always taking notes, writing little phrases that I think might work. Songs come easy sometimes and sometimes they don't. I've tried to arrive at formulas for turning out songs, but they didn't work. Sometimes the music comes first and sometimes the words come first."

—JOHN HARTFORD

HAMBURGER CASSEROLE FOR A CROWD

3 lb. ground beef or chuck
1 jar (8 oz.) Cheez Whiz
1 carton (16 oz.) sour cream
4 lg. onions, chopped
1 lb. sharp cheese, grated
1½ lb. noodles (½ inch), cooked and drained
1 can (10¾ oz.) cream of mushroom soup
2 lg. cans tomato sauce

- Brown meat with onions. Add soup, Cheez Whiz, grated cheese, tomato sauce, and sour cream. Let simmer. Add noodles and mix well.
- Put into large baking dish. Sprinkle a little grated cheese on top. Bake at 400 degrees until bubbly.

Prepared for crew at Country Fest.

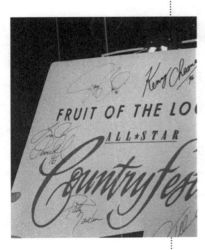

"When I first started learning how to write, teaching myself and studying everybody else's style, it was so much easier to work from the emotional side. Country music is based on strong emotional type things and it's more natural. There is an emotional side to everybody alive. There are just different levels of intensity."

—EARL THOMAS CONLEY

VEGETABLE-BEEF CASSEROLE

1 lb. ground beef
1 lg. onion, chopped
1 can mixed vegetables
1 can (10¾ oz.) cream of
    mushroom soup
1 cup buttered bread
    crumbs

- Brown beef and onion; place over vegetables in casserole. Cover with soup; top with crumbs. Bake at 350 degrees for 30 minutes.

YIELDS 6 SERVINGS.

Prepared for George Strait.

"**W**riting is like genius, it is ninety percent perspiration and ten percent inspiration. It really is."

—JOE DIFFIE

Zucchini and Tomato Casserole

2–4 zucchini squash
2–4 lg. tomatoes
  1 red onion
     salt and pepper
  1 pkg. instant potatoes
  1 cup catsup
     buttered bread crumbs

• Boil squash, tomatoes, and onion together for several minutes or until squash is tender. Place in casserole; add seasoning, potatoes, and catsup. Top with crumbs. Bake at 350 degrees for 15 minutes.

YIELDS 8 SERVINGS.

Prepared for Hal Ketchum.

"**I** always try to write from a realistic point of view, whether it's a good or a bad situation. I always include a glimmer of hope in every situation. With faith and a little persistence, there is always a little window open somewhere. Sometimes you just have to look a little harder."

—LEROY PARNELL

VEGETARIAN BROCCOLI CASSEROLE

3 pkg. (10 oz.) frozen chopped broccoli
1 can (10¾ oz.) cream of mushroom soup
3 tsp. onion, grated
½ cup mayonnaise
3 eggs, well beaten
¾ cup Ritz crackers, crushed

- Cook broccoli 5 minutes. Drain and spread in bottom of 2 or 3 quart casserole.
- Mix soup, onion, mayonnaise, eggs, and pour over broccoli in the casserole. Sprinkle cracker crumbs on top.
- Bake 20 to 30 minutes at 350 degrees. Casserole may be assembled ahead of time, refrigerated, and baked just prior to serving.

YIELDS 10 SERVINGS.

Prepared for Hal Ketchum.

> **"I** write about how people are living. This way, I know it's going to touch people. It's got to touch people, because I'm just like they are, and if it touches me, it has to touch them, too."
>
> —LORETTA LYNN

BROCCOLI CASSEROLE

1 pkg. (10 oz.) frozen broccoli, chopped
½ can cream of mushroom soup
½ cup mayonnaise
1 egg, beaten well
½ cup cheese, grated
2 tbsp. onion, chopped
2 tbsp. butter
¼ cup crackers, crushed

- Cook broccoli in salt water according to instructions on package.
- In separate bowl, mix soup, mayonnaise, egg, cheese, onion, and salt and pepper to taste. Add cooked broccoli. Spoon into lightly greased casserole dish. Dot with butter. Sprinkle with crushed crackers.
- Bake at 350 degrees for 30 to 40 minutes.

Prepared for Shelly West.

"I like to write songs that paint pictures. You paint a different picture with a video. That's what I like about videos."

—DARON NORWOOD

VEGETABLE CASSEROLE FOR CREW

1 can peas
1 can asparagus
1 can green beans, French-cut
1 can (10¾ oz.) of mushroom soup
¼ cup milk
½ cup almonds, sliced
¼ cup stuffed olives, sliced
¼ cup cheese, grated
1 pkg. (8 oz.) frozen onion rings

- Drain peas, asparagus, and beans. Combine all ingredients except cheese and onion rings in 3-quart casserole.
- Bake at 350 degrees for 20 minutes. Add cheese and onion rings; bake for 15 minutes longer.

YIELDS 12 SERVINGS.

Prepared for crew at Country Fest.

"**I** think I've always looked for songs from a songwriter's point of view, since I'm a songwriter myself. I'm a soul type of singer. I sing from the heart."

—JOHN ANDERSON

ASPARAGUS-EGG CASSEROLE

1 tbsp. parsley, chopped
½ cup American cheese, grated
2 cups med. white sauce
1 pkg. (12 oz.) frozen asparagus, cooked
1 cup string beans, cooked
1 cup whole kernel corn, cooked
4 eggs, hard-cooked and sliced
  bread crumbs
  salt to taste

• Blend salt, parsley, and cheese with white sauce. Layer in buttered 2-quart casserole with asparagus, beans, corn, and eggs. Sprinkle with bread crumbs.
• Bake at 325 degrees for 30 minutes.

YIELDS 6 SERVINGS.

Prepared for Barbara Mandrell.

"**Y**ou can approach song writing as a craft and probably make a living doing it. It's a different story to explore your own emotions and put them in perspective—taking it from your soul, to your mind, to your pencil, and out to the world."

—HAL KETCHUM

CHEESY ASPARAGUS AND PEAS CASSEROLE

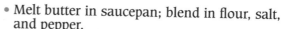

2 tbsp. butter
2 tbsp. flour
½ tsp. salt
¼ tsp. pepper
1 egg, beaten
1½ cup milk
¼ tsp. cinnamon
1 pkg. frozen
    asparagus, cooked
1 pkg. frozen peas,
    cooked
1 cup cheese, grated
½ cup buttered bread
    crumbs
    paprika

- Melt butter in saucepan; blend in flour, salt, and pepper.
- Combine egg and milk; gradually add to flour mixture, stirring constantly. Cook and stir until thick. Add cinnamon.
- Alternate layers of asparagus and peas in oiled casserole dish. Pour sauce over vegetables. Top with cheese and bread crumbs.
- Bake at 350 degrees for 20 to 25 minutes. Garnish with paprika.

NOTE:
Cheese may be cut in wedges instead of grated.

YIELDS 8 SERVINGS.

Prepared for Billy Dean.

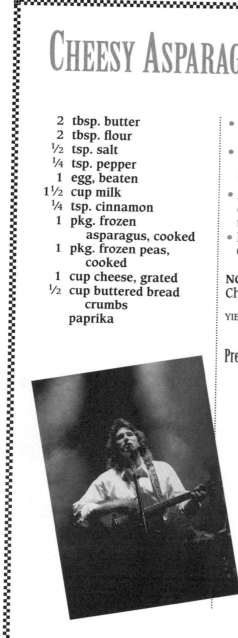

"**I** believe that each song should reveal something about the entertainer that hasn't been told before. I think the artist owes that to the fans. I admire James Taylor because he has the ability to say things in ways that I have never thought of before."

—GARTH BROOKS

Broccoli and Peas Casserole

1 cup cream of
    mushroom soup
1 sm. jar Cheez Whiz
    liquid from cooked
    vegetables
1 pkg. frozen peas,
    cooked
1 pkg. frozen broccoli,
    cooked
2–3 tbsp. melted butter
¾ cup cracker or bread
    crumbs

- Heat soup with Cheez Whiz and liquid from vegetables until melted and blended. Add vegetables and heat. Place in greased 8-inch baking dish. Top with mixture of butter and crumbs.
- Bake at 325 to 350 degrees for 30 minutes.

YIELDS 6–8 SERVINGS.

Prepared for Charlie Walker.

"My basic criteria for a good country song is that the lyrical content is something that is going to move people, one way or another. I can't see longevity in any song with bubble gum lyrics."

—Suzy Bogguss

BROCCOLI AND CAULIFLOWER CASSEROLE

1 pkg. (10 oz.) frozen
  cauliflower
1 pkg. (10 oz.) frozen
  chopped broccoli
1 can (10¾ oz.) cream
  of asparagus soup
1 can (10¾ oz.) cream
  of celery soup
1 carton (8 oz.) sour cream
  sharp cheese, grated

- Cook broccoli and cauliflower by package directions. Drain. Mix all ingredients except cheese. Put in a 1½-quart casserole dish. Grate cheese and sprinkle on top.
- Bake at 350 degrees for 20 to 25 minutes.

Prepared for The Statler Brothers.

> **"I** grew up in a small town listening to great story tellers. Their influence makes some of my songs just 'fall from the sky.'"
>
> —HAL KETCHUM

CASSEROLE SPAGHETTI

1½ lbs. ground chuck
1 bell pepper, chopped
1 lg. onion, chopped
½ cup celery, chopped
2 cloves garlic (may use
    garlic salt)
1 can (10¾ oz.) cream of
    mushroom soup
½ can water
1 can (16 oz.) tomatoes
2 tablespoons chili
    powder
    salt and pepper to taste
1 pkg. (6 to 8 oz.)
    spaghetti noodles
½ cup sharp cheese,
    in chunks
1 jar (4 oz.) olives
¾ cup cheese, grated

- Brown ground chuck. Add next 9 ingredients and simmer 2 hours.
- Cook spaghetti according to package directions.
- Combine meat sauce, spaghetti, chunks of cheese, and olives in 3-quart casserole dish. Sprinkle grated cheese on top.
- Bake in 325 degree oven for 15 to 20 minutes or until bubbly.

YIELDS 6 SERVINGS.

Prepared for Bryan White.

"I'm in country music because the song writing is the most interesting and the most exciting of any music. The song writing community in Nashville is the best in the world."

—LARI WHITE

SENATOR THOMPSON'S SWEET POTATO CASSEROLE

3 cups sweet potatoes,
   cooked and mashed
1 cup sugar
2 eggs
1 tbsp. vanilla extract
½ cup butter, melted

- Mix sweet potatoes, sugar, eggs, vanilla, and butter thoroughly. Pour into buttered 1-quart casserole.

TOPPING

1 cup brown sugar, packed
½ cup flour
1 cup chopped nuts
⅓ cup butter

- Mix all the topping ingredients together with a fork. Sprinkle the crumbs on top of the casserole.
- Bake for 30 minutes at 350 degrees.

YIELDS 8 SERVINGS.

Prepared for Ty England.

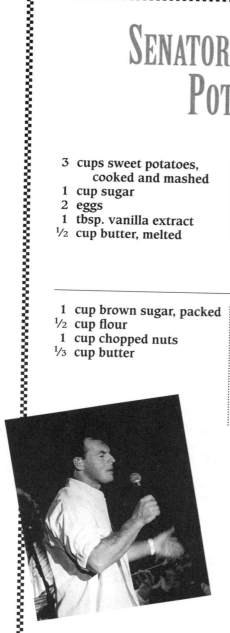

"I enjoy writing a song, putting the music, taking it into the studio, recording and getting the song out to the people. That's a good feeling."

—VERN GOSDIN

VIDALIA ONION CASSEROLE

2 tbsp. butter or
   margarine
2 tbsp. flour
1 cup chicken broth
   or
1 chicken bouillon cube in
   1 cup water
1 can (5⅛ oz.)
   evaporated milk
3 cups wedged Vidalia
   onions, parboiled
½ cup almonds, slivered
½ tsp. salt
½ tsp. pepper
1 cup bread crumbs
½ cup cheese, grated

- Melt butter; stir in flour, then all broth and evaporated milk. Stir constantly until mixture begins to thicken and is smooth.
- Add drained onions, almonds, and seasonings. Pour into buttered 1½-quart casserole. Cover with crumbs and cheese.
- Bake at 375 degrees for 30 minutes.

NOTE:
Vidalia onions are very mild, sweet onions grown exclusively in sandy soil near Vidalia, Georgia. They are usually available from late spring through mid-summer. Any sweet type of onion could be substituted.

Prepared for Sammy Kershaw.

"**E**very story has been written. There's nothing new. I look for a song that says something, but in a little bit of a different way. The song should be written to say what it's going to say in a little bit of a different way to catch the attention of the buying public."

—LEROY VAN DYKE

Mama's Favorite Pork Chop Casserole

1 pkg. (6 oz.) long-grain and wild rice mix
2 cups hot water
6 bone-in pork loin chops, trimmed
¼ teaspoon pepper
1 can (10¾ oz.) cream of celery soup, undiluted
½ cup milk

- Combine rice mix with hot water according to directions on package. Place in a greased 13×9×2 inch baking dish. Set aside.
- Sprinkle pork chops with pepper, and place atop rice mixture.
- Cover and bake at 350 degrees for one hour. Uncover casserole.
- Combine cream of celery soup and milk, and pour over casserole. Bake uncovered for 15 minutes or until thoroughly heated.

Prepared for Colin Raye.

"You can have the best talents in the world at your feet but if you don't have the right song to showcase them, you really don't have a chance."

—Bryan White

Part Five

VEGETABLES

Bob's Barbecued Beans

½ lb. ground beef
½ cup onion, chopped
⅓ cup sugar
⅓ cup brown sugar
½ cup barbecue sauce
¼ cup ketchup
½ tsp. salt
½ tsp. pepper
½ tsp. chili powder
2 tbsp. molasses
2 tsp. Dijon mustard
1 can (15 oz.) kidney
      beans
1 can (15 oz.) butter
      beans
1 can (16 oz.) pork & beans
10 slices of bacon, cooked
      and crumbled

- Drain kidney and butter beans.
- Cook ground beef and chopped onions, stirring until meat crumbles. Drain beef mixture and place in large bowl.
- Stir sugar and remaining ingredients into mixture. Spoon into a greased 2½-quart baking dish. Bake uncovered at 350 degrees for one hour, stirring once.

Prepared for Ken Mellons.

"I never have reservations singing any song that speaks truly about today's times."

—Patty Loveless

Henry's Baked Beans

1 lb. ground beef
1 pkg. (1½ oz.) dry onion soup mix
1 can (8 oz.) tomato sauce
2 cans (16 oz.) pork and beans
1 can (16 oz.) kidney beans
2 tbsp. prepared mustard
2 tsp. cider vinegar

- Cook beef and soup mix in 10-inch casserole dish in microwave oven on 100% power for 5 to 6 minutes; drain.
- Add remaining ingredients, mix well.
- Cook in microwave oven at 100% power for 6 to 8 minutes more.

Prepared for Daryle Singletary.

"**I** don't hesitate to go out on a limb if something seems right."

—Shelly West

TEXAS BAKED BEANS

½ lb. ground beef
2 cans (16 oz.) pork and beans
1 can (15¾ oz.) barbecued beans
1 med. onion, chopped
½ cup green pepper, chopped
½ cup brown sugar, firmly packed
¼ cup molasses
¼ cup catsup
2 tbsp. prepared mustard
1 tbsp. Worcestershire sauce
1 clove garlic, crushed
1 tsp. seasoned salt
½ tsp. lemon-pepper seasoning
4–5 slices bacon

- Cook ground beef until browned; then drain well.
- Combine all ingredients except bacon, and mix well; pour into a 13×9×2 inch baking dish. Top with bacon.
- Bake at 350 degrees for 2 hours.

YIELDS 8 SERVINGS.

Prepared for George Strait.

"I have a hard time doing gospel songs. I would much rather record songs like 'The River' and 'Unanswered Prayers' and others songs that let people know that I know that God exists."

—GARTH BROOKS

CROWD-PLEASING BAKED BEANS

2 lbs. Great Northern
dried beans
1 cup brown sugar, firmly
packed
½ cup molasses
1 tbsp. + 1 tsp. dry
mustard
1 tbsp. salt
1 lg. onion, chopped
1½ lbs. slab bacon, cut into
1-inch squares

- Sort and wash beans; place in a Dutch oven. Cover with water 2 inches above beans; let soak overnight. Cover and bring to a boil; reduce heat, and simmer 45 minutes. Drain, reserving liquid. Add enough water to bean liquid to make 1¾ cups; set aside.
- Combine brown sugar, molasses, mustard, and salt; stir well.
- Layer half of beans, brown sugar mixture, onion, and bacon in a 4½-quart casserole. Top with remaining beans. Pour reserved bean liquid over top.
- Cover and bake at 300 degree for 5 hours.

YIELDS 20–22 SERVINGS.

Prepared for Fan Fair picnic.

"For a few years, as a teenager, I listened to rock music but I think it lacked that personal touch. Realism in country music is that heart that lives inside you."

—JAMES BONAMY

NEW ORLEANS RED BEANS

1 lb. red kidney beans, dried
salt to taste
1 clove garlic, finely chopped
1 med. onion, finely chopped
3–4 stalks of celery, finely chopped
24 inches of link sausage
3 bay leaves
4 pieces of ham hock
6–7 cups of water

- Wash 1 pound of red kidney beans and put into large pot with salt to taste.
- Brown sausage links and cut into small pieces.
- In separate skillet, sauté garlic, onion, and celery and add to beans. Add browned sausage, bay leaves, ham hock pieces, and 6 or 7 cups of water.
- Cover and cook over low heat for 2 to 2½ hours.

NOTE:
This may be served with rice and can be a protein substitute for a main course of meat.

Prepared for Sammy Kershaw.

"**I** would like to be the vehicle to pull young people into country music. I would rather for them to listen to country music than music that has violence and stuff that leads them in the wrong direction."

—BRYAN WHITE

Fresh Lima Beans and Scallions

3 cups lima beans, shelled fresh
5 sm. scallions or green onions
3 tbsp. butter or margarine, melted
1 tbsp. all-purpose flour
½ tsp. salt
¼ tsp. white pepper
¼ tsp. paprika

- Cook beans in boiling salted water 20 minutes or until tender; drain, reserving ½ cup liquid.
- Cut scallions in ½-inch pieces and sauté scallions in butter until tender. Add flour, stirring until smooth. Cook 1 minute, stirring constantly. Gradually stir in reserved liquid; cook over medium heat, stirring constantly until thickened.
- Stir in lima beans, salt, pepper, and paprika.

YIELDS 4–6 SERVINGS.

Prepared for Daryle Singletary.

"**I**f your sound is unique, you can have your own space as long as you have commercially appealing music that radio feels comfortable playing."
—Dave Robbins

COUNTRY MASHED POTATOES

2 cups mashed potatoes
½ cup milk
2 tbsp. butter
1 tsp. salt
    dash of pepper
2 eggs (separated)
½ cup sharp Cheddar
    cheese (2 oz.),
    shredded

- Combine first 5 ingredients; beat at medium speed of electric mixer until smooth.
- Beat egg yolks until thick; stir yolks and cheese into potato mixture.
- Beat egg whites (at room temperature) until stiff but not dry; gently fold into potato mixture. Spoon into a greased 1-quart casserole dish.
- Cover and bake at 350 degrees for 20 to 25 minutes.

YIELDS 4 SERVINGS.

Prepared for Johnny Wright.

"Radio programmers are turned on to the cutting edge or hot country sounds. Wake up! We baby boomers love the retro Patsy Cline sound. There is a market out there for that sound. These new kids need and can be turned on to these classic country sounds. We can not go forward without looking back."

—RONNIE McDOWELL

GRANDPA'S SWEET POTATO SOUFFLE

3 cups sweet potatoes,
   cooked and mashed
1 cup sugar
¼ cup milk
2 eggs
1 tsp. vanilla
½ cup (1 stick) butter,
   melted
⅓ cup all-purpose flour
1 tsp. orange peel, grated
2 tbsp. fresh orange juice

- In a mixing bowl, combine sweet potatoes, sugar, milk, eggs, vanilla, melted butter, flour, orange peel, and orange juice. Mix well and pour into a greased 2-quart baking or souffle dish.

TOPPING

1 cup pecans, chopped
1 cup brown sugar
½ cup (1 stick) butter,
   melted
⅓ cup all-purpose flour

- Combine topping ingredients in a small bowl and scatter over sweet potato mixture. Reserve several pecan halves for garnish, if desired.
- Bake at 350 degrees for 40 minutes, or until bubbly.

YIELDS 8 SERVINGS.

Prepared for Grandpa Jones.

"Consistency, attention to detail, and the careful selection of songs are important in the longevity of a career."

—HENRY PAUL

BOURBON SWEET POTATOES

6–8 sweet potatoes
      or
  1 can (30 oz.), drained
  2 eggs
  6 tbsp. margarine,
      melted
  1 cup brown sugar
  3 tbsp. bourbon
 ⅓ cup sweetened
      condensed milk
  1 can (8 oz.) crushed
      pineapple with juice

- If using raw sweet potatoes, cook, peel, and mash. Put potatoes, eggs, margarine, sugar, bourbon, and condensed milk in blender. Blend well. If using canned potatoes, there will be some lumps.
- Add pineapple last to avoid liquefying. Pour into 2-quart oblong casserole and top with cereal mixture.
- Bake at 375 degrees for 20 minutes until set.

TOPPING

  2 cups Grape-Nuts
      (cereal)
 ⅓ cup nuts, chopped
 ¼ cup margarine, melted

- Mix dry ingredients. Add melted margarine and stir well.

YIELDS 10–12 SERVINGS.

Prepared for Ty England.

> "The hardest part is to believe in yourself, to continue to be objective, and to hang in there."
> —HOLLY DUNN

CREAMY FRIED TOMATOES

6	lg. tomatoes
3	tbsp. flour
1½	tsp. salt
⅛	tsp. pepper
¼	cup butter
1½	cup milk
1½	tsp. sugar
¾	tsp. bottled thick meat sauce
1½	tsp. mustard

- Core tomatoes; half crosswise.
- Combine 1 tablespoon flour, ¾ teaspoon salt and pepper; sprinkle over tomatoes. Sauté in butter until tender; arrange 10 halves on heated platter.
- To remaining tomato halves, add remaining flour and salt, milk, sugar, meat sauce, and mustard; cook until thickened, stirring constantly. Pour over tomatoes; serve for breakfast or lunch, plain or on toast.

YIELDS 5 SERVINGS.

Prepared for Doug Stone.

"I don't want to ever look at myself in the mirror and ask what might have happened if I had applied myself and tried something."

—TRACE ATKINS

FRIED GREEN TOMATOES

4 lg. green tomatoes
2 cups plain corn meal
1½ tbsp. salt
   pinch of black pepper
½ cup shortening or
   cooking oil

- Wash the tomatoes and pat dry. Cut tomatoes in ¼-inch slices. Sprinkle with salt and pepper. Dip each slice into corn meal and lay aside on waxed paper.
- Heat oil. Fry tomato slices until golden brown. Drain on paper towels. Serve hot.

YIELDS 4 SERVINGS.

Prepared for Marty Raybon.

"If it is to be, it's up to me."

—RONNIE MCDOWELL

Dottie's Green Tomatoes

4–5 med. green tomatoes
⅓ cup flour
¾ tsp. salt
    few grains of pepper
    (optional)
¼ cup shortening

- Wash tomatoes; remove stem end. Cut cross-wise into ½-inch slices.
- Blend flour, salt, and pepper; dip tomato slices into mixture. Brown quickly in fat on one side; turn. Reduce heat; cook until soft in center. Remove to hot platter; serve hot.

YIELDS 4–5 SERVINGS.

Prepared for Dottie West.

"I believe you are supposed to experience all of life without hurting anybody else. There are good sides and bad sides, and I like to express both of these, and there's a powerful message in the most intense things I do."

—EARL THOMAS CONLEY

STUFFED GREEN PEPPERS AND TOMATOES

6 tbsp. fat
1 sm. onion, minced
1 cup celery, diced
9 slices day-old bread, cubed
1 tsp. salt
1 tsp. pepper
1 tsp. thyme
3 tomatoes
3 green peppers

- Melt fat; add onion and celery and sauté for 10 minutes or until tender. Add bread cubes and seasonings; mix well. Add enough water to soften bread mixture; toss with a fork until well blended.
- Scoop out tomatoes and peppers; fill with stuffing.
- Bake at 350 degrees until done.

YIELDS 6 SERVINGS.

Prepared for Marty Robbins.

"**I** know where I came from, so I know where I have been. If I can remember this, I can always know where I am going."
—SAMMY KERSHAW

SPICED CHERRY TOMATOES

1½ pts. cherry tomatoes
½ cup soft bread crumbs
¼ cup + 2 tbsp. onion, minced
¼ cup + 2 tbsp. fresh parsley, minced
2 tbsp. olive oil
1 lg. clove garlic, minced
½ tsp. dried whole thyme
¼ tsp. salt
⅛ tsp. pepper

- Place tomatoes in an 8-inch baking dish.
- Combine remaining ingredients, stirring well; spoon over tomatoes.
- Bake at 425 degrees for 6 to 8 minutes.

YIELDS 6 SERVINGS.

Prepared for Hal Ketchum.

"I have certain fundamentals I use to guide my life; therefore, when you buy my music you are also buying who I am as a total person."

—JAMES BONAMY

MARINATED TOMATO SLICES

4 tomatoes, sliced
1 onion, thinly sliced
1 cup vegetable oil
⅓ cup wine vinegar
⅛ tsp. garlic powder
  salt and pepper
  lettuce leaves
    (optional)

- Arrange tomato and onion slices in a shallow container.
- Combine oil, vinegar, and garlic powder; stir well, and pour over tomato and onion. Sprinkle with salt and pepper.
- Cover and marinate in refrigerator at least 10 minutes. Serve over lettuce leaves, if desired.

YIELDS 8 SERVINGS.

Prepared for Ken Mellons.

"**W**hen I first came to Nashville, I know I took real chances because I was so intense about pursuing my career. I really had blinders on. When I was younger, I took a leap of faith in many instances that I might not take today."

—TERI CLARK

JUNIOR'S FRIED CORN

8 ears tender corn
¼ cup bacon drippings
1 cup milk
   salt and pepper to taste
1 tsp. sugar
1 tbsp. butter

- Cut corn close to outer edge, then scrape the ear to remove all the milk. Add corn to bacon drippings which have been heated. Add milk, salt, pepper, and sugar.
- Stir often as corn burns easily. Cook approximately 20 to 30 minutes, adding butter during the last few minutes of cooking.

Prepared for Loretta Lynn.

"**I** like romantic songs. When I first started to make records I saw myself singing romantic songs. I think people crave something that takes them away from what they are experiencing in everyday life. People need to fantasize and forget their troubles for a little while."

—SUZY BOGGUSS

SEASONED BAKED CORN ON THE COB

4 ears fresh corn
¼ cup + 1 tbsp. butter or
       margarine, softened
½ tsp. freeze-dried chives
¼ tsp. salt
¼ tsp. prepared mustard
⅛ tsp. pepper

- Remove husks and silks from corn just before cooking.
- Combine remaining ingredients, stirring well. Spread herb butter on corn, place each ear on a piece of aluminum foil; wrap tightly.
- Bake at 400 degrees for 45 minutes, turning occasionally.

YIELDS 4 SERVINGS.

Prepared for Tracy Byrd.

"**I**f I have not lived the song, I can't put my heart into it. I think the fans can detect when you're singing from the heart and mean what you're singing or if you're faking it. I don't want to be a fake about anything."

—SAMMY KERSHAW

SOUTHERN FRIED OKRA

2 lbs. small okra
1 cup plain corn meal
1 cup all-purpose flour
1½ qts. vegetable oil, for
deep frying

- Wash okra and cut into fairly thin slices; do not use stem or tip. Make sure okra is moist with water, and place in large plastic container with a lid.
- Add meal and flour. Place lid on container and shake several times. Remove lid and make sure all okra slices are coated with meal-flour mixture.
- Fry coated okra slices in deep vegetable oil until brown. Remove with slotted spoon and drain on paper towel. Salt to taste while hot.

Prepared for Charlie Daniels.

"**I** like to sing songs that don't require me to garner any false emotions. I try to sing songs that mean something to me."

—DOUG SUPERNAW

SPINACH BALLS

2 boxes frozen spinach, chopped
2 cups herb stuffing mix
2 onions, chopped fine
6 eggs, beaten
¾ cup butter, melted
½ cup Parmesan cheese
1 tbsp. garlic salt
½ tsp. thyme
½ tsp. pepper
1 tsp. MSG (monosodium glutamate)

- Cook spinach and drain well. Add all ingredients mixing thoroughly. Roll into balls. Refrigerate overnight if possible.
- Bake 20 minutes at 350 degrees.

Prepared for CMA post awards party.

> "I knew when I started I couldn't do what everyone else was doing. I wanted to do real good, feel good music. I grew up listening to Chuck Berry, Jerry Lee Lewis, Elvis, Johnny Cash, Johnny Horton, and people like that. That's what I wanted to do. I'm still doing what I started out doing."
>
> —MEL MCDANIEL

SQUASH BALLS

8 sm. yellow squash
  pepper to taste
2 tbsp. butter
1 tsp. chicken bouillon
1 sm. onion, chopped fine
1 egg, beaten
3 cups stuffing mix
1 cup Cheddar cheese,
  shredded

- Cook squash until tender, drain well and mash. Add pepper, butter, bouillon, and onion.
- Mix egg and stuffing mix, saving 1 cup aside for later use. Add cheese and mix all ingredients together well. Let stand about 10 minutes for stuffing to soften. Roll into balls. Makes about 50.
- Place remainder of stuffing into blender and blend until fine. Roll balls in crumbs.
- Spray cookie sheet with vegetable spray and bake 20 to 25 minutes at 350 degrees. Serve warm or cold. Can be frozen for later use.

Prepared for CMA post awards party.

"I've always thought of myself as someone who is outside the parameters of what people expect. I have a lot of energy and I use this energy to entertain an audience. You have to create show business—you can't let it come to you—you have to create it."

—LEE GREENWOOD

CHEESY STUFFED SQUASH

6 med. yellow squash
½ lb. bacon
1 sm. onion, chopped
¾ cup soft bread crumbs
1 cup sharp Cheddar
    cheese (4 ounces),
    shredded
paprika
fresh parsley (optional)

- Wash squash thoroughly; cover with salted water and boil 8 to 10 minutes or until tender but still firm. Drain and cool slightly. Remove and discard stems. Cut in half lengthwise; remove and reserve pulp, leaving a firm shell.
- Cook bacon in a large skillet until crisp; drain well, reserving 2 tablespoons bacon drippings in skillet. Crumble bacon, and set aside.
- Sauté onion in bacon drippings until tender; stir in bacon, bread crumbs, and squash pulp.
- Place squash shells in a 13×9×2 inch baking dish. Spoon squash mixture into shells; top with cheese. Broil 6 inches from heat about 5 minutes or just until cheese is melted. Sprinkle with paprika. Garnish with parsley, if desired.

YIELDS 6 SERVINGS.

Prepared for Ty England.

"At a live performance, you get feedback immediately. You know when something is working—the audience tells you right away. Sometimes it takes years for the songwriter to get the recognition back.

—HOLLY DUNN

SQUASH DRESSING

$\frac{1}{2}$ cup onion, chopped
$\frac{1}{2}$ green pepper, chopped
$\frac{1}{2}$ cup celery, chopped
$\frac{1}{2}$ cup margarine or
    butter, melted
5 cups corn bread
2 cups fresh milk
1 can ($10\frac{3}{4}$ oz.) cream
    of chicken soup
3 cups yellow squash,
    cooked
1 tsp. salt
$\frac{1}{4}$ tsp. pepper

- Cook squash until tender; chop and drain.
- Sauté first four ingredients until tender. Add corn bread and stir; mix other ingredients and pour into a greased 13×9×2 inch baking pan.
- Bake at 400 degrees for 50 minutes or until light brown.

Prepared for Pee Wee King.

"The really good feel- ing that comes to me is when I do concerts and I see little kids singing the words of my song with me. That's the big thrill for me. The rest of it is a business."

—JOHNNY LEE

SPICED CARROTS

1 lb. sm. carrots, scraped
⅓ cup orange juice
   concentrate, thawed
⅓ cup hot water
1 lemon, thin sliced
1 tsp. onion, grated
2 tsp. brown sugar
½ tsp. salt
   dash of white pepper
1 1-in. piece of stick
   cinnamon
2 whole cloves
2 whole allspice berries
   several blades of whole
   mace
2 tbsp. butter or
   margarine

- Place carrots in large, heavy skillet or saucepan.
- Mix remaining ingredients; pour over carrots. Cover tightly and bring to a boil. Simmer for 20 minutes or until carrots are tender.
- Remove spices before serving.

YIELDS 6 SERVINGS.

Prepared for Alabama.

"When I do a show I want to stand up there and sing so that when the show's over you will be able to say, 'I know something about that guy. I know what he thinks is funny, I know what he thinks is offensive, what he likes, and what he doesn't like.'"

—DANNY SHIRLEY

SWEET-AND-SOUR CARROTS

1 lb. carrots, scraped and diagonally sliced
1 med. green pepper, chopped
⅓ cup sugar
1 tsp. cornstarch
½ tsp. salt
1 can (8 oz.) pineapple chunks
2 tsp. vinegar
2 tsp. soy sauce

- In a covered saucepan, cook carrots until tender in a small amount of boiling salted water. Add green pepper and cook 3 minutes. Drain and set aside.
- Combine sugar, cornstarch, and salt in a medium saucepan.
- Drain pineapple and combine juice with enough water to make ⅓ cup liquid; stir into sugar mixture. Stir in vinegar and soy sauce; cook over low heat until bubbly, stirring constantly.
- Stir in vegetables and pineapple; cook until well heated.

YIELDS 6–8 SERVINGS.

Prepared for The Gatlins.

"**I**'m happiest when I am on stage. Except for the time I spend with my children, that ninety minutes of show time that I get to do is what I live for."
—TRACE ATKINS

SAVORY STUFFED MUSHROOMS

2 tbsp. butter or margarine
¼ cup onion, chopped
1 clove garlic, finely chopped
1 cup cottage cheese
1–2 tsp. seasoned salt
1 cup herb-seasoned stuffing mix
4 slices bacon
18–24 lg. fresh mushroom caps
melted butter
pimento strips

- Preheat oven to 350 degrees.
- Fry bacon until crisp. Crumble and set aside.
- In a small skillet, melt butter or margarine. Add onion and garlic and cook until tender.
- In a large bowl, mix together cottage cheese and seasoned salt. Stir in stuffing mix, bacon, and onion.
- Brush mushrooms with melted butter or margarine; fill with stuffing mixture, mounding slightly. Garnish with pimento strips.
- Place in a shallow baking dish and bake 10–12 minutes. Serve hot.

Prepared for CMA post awards party.

"At concerts, my band and I know that we're not the best pickers or the best singers in the world. People see with their eyes and hear with their eyes. So it's much more important that we enjoy ourselves on stage. If we're doing a ballad, we show our emotions with our actions. We could hit a bad note, I could sing flat or I could sing sharp, but those people aren't caring because they really are hearing with their eyes. So you must get through to the people with your actions."

—NEAL McCoy

Part Six

DESSERTS

Sweet Potato Pie

1½ cups sugar
3 eggs
1½ cups mashed sweet
   potatoes
1 tsp. vanilla extract
1 stick butter, melted
½ cup milk
1 deep 9-inch pie shell,
   unbaked

- Beat together sugar and eggs. Add potatoes, vanilla extract, and melted butter and mix. Then add milk.
- Cook in unbaked pie shell for 1 hour at 350 degrees.

Prepared for Eddie Rabbitt.

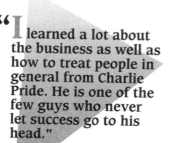

"I learned a lot about the business as well as how to treat people in general from Charlie Pride. He is one of the few guys who never let success go to his head."

—Neal McCoy

EASY COCONUT PIE I

6	eggs
1⅓	cups buttermilk
3	cups sugar
1½	sticks margarine, melted
1	pkg. (14 oz.) angel flake coconut
1	tsp. vanilla extract
¼	tsp. salt
3	unbaked pie shells (8- or 9-inch) whipping cream, whipped and sweetened

- Beat eggs very well. Add remaining ingredients one at a time and blend well after each addition. Pour into three unbaked pie shells.
- Bake at 325 degrees for 40 to 45 minutes. Cool and serve topped with a dollop of sweetened whipped cream.

NOTE:
Pies freeze well after baking.

Prepared for Hal Ketchum.

"**M**ickey Gilley told me how important it is to be friendly with all your fans. They're the people who come to see us; they're the people who keep us going."

—JOHNNY LEE

SOUTHERN PECAN PIE I

1 cup brown sugar
2 tbsp. flour
1½ tbsp. butter
1 cup light corn syrup
3 eggs, beaten
¼ tsp. salt
1 tsp. vanilla extract
1½–2 cups pecans
1 unbaked pie shell
(9-inch)

- Allow butter to soften at room temperature.
- Mix sugar and flour. Cream butter with sugar and flour mixture. Add corn syrup and eggs. Beat with mixer until frothy. Add salt, vanilla, and pecans. Pour into unbaked pie shell.
- Bake 45 minutes at 325 degrees.

Prepared for Shelly West.

"My first job on the road was with Faron Young. He taught me so much, especially to be less shy and talk to people."

—DARRELL McCALL

SOUTHERN PECAN PIE II

3 lg. eggs
1 cup white corn syrup
¾ cup sugar
1 tbsp. orange juice
2 tbsp. orange rind, grated
2 tbsp. butter, melted
1 cup pecans, coarsely
   chopped
1 pie shell, unbaked
   whipped cream,
   optional

- Beat eggs slightly. Add syrup, sugar, juice, and rind. Stir in butter. Spread pecans over unbaked pie crust and pour filling over.
- Bake approximately 45 minutes at 350 degrees. Serve topped with whipped cream, if desired.

YIELDS 1 (8- OR 9-INCH) PIE.

Prepared for Charlie Walker.

"I've learned from Randy Travis that you can be successful and humble at the same time."

—DARYLE SINGLETARY

BLUE MOON OF KENTUCKY BUTTERMILK PIE

3¾ cup granulated sugar
½ cup flour
½ tsp. salt
6 eggs
1 cup buttermilk
1 tsp. vanilla
1 cup butter, melted
1 tsp. butter flavoring
  (if using margarine)
  optional
2 8-inch unbaked pie
  shells
  or
1 10-inch unbaked pie
  shell

• Mix sugar, flour, and salt in bowl. Add eggs, stirring just enough to break them up. Add buttermilk and vanilla. Stir until just blended. Add melted butter. Stir slightly and quickly.
• Pour into pie shells, bake at 350 degrees 45 to 50 minutes, or until center is set. Cool thoroughly before cutting. (Pies may be frozen weeks or months before using. Allow one full day for thawing in refrigerator).

Prepared for Bill Monroe.

"I never go on stage with a song set. We just wing it. We're kinda like the Grateful Dead of country. I don't want to be the star on stage. I just kinda want to be the host of the party."

—DOUG SUPERNAW

BLACKBERRY COBBLER

FILLING

5 cups fresh blackberries
¾ cup sugar
1 tbsp. cornstarch
⅛ tsp. salt
2 tbsp. butter or
    margarine
    pastry (recipe follows)
1 tbsp. milk
1 tbsp. sugar
    vanilla ice cream

- Wash berries thoroughly, and drain well; place in a 9-inch-square baking dish. Combine ¾ cup sugar, cornstarch, and salt; sprinkle mixture over berries. Dot with butter.
- Roll pastry out on a lightly floured surface into a 9-inch square; place over berries, sealing edges to sides of dish. Cut slits in crust. Brush crust with milk, and sprinkle with 1 tablespoon sugar.
- Bake at 425 degrees for 30 minutes or until crust is golden brown. Serve with vanilla ice cream.

YIELDS 6 SERVINGS.

PASTRY

1 cup all-purpose flour
½ tsp. salt
⅓ cup shortening
2 tbsp. cold water

- Combine flour and salt. Cut in shortening until mixture resembles coarse crumbs; sprinkle with water, and stir with a fork until mixture forms a ball. Yields enough for one 9-inch cobbler or a 1-crust pie.

Prepared for Janie Fricke.

"**I** don't do a play list because I like to keep me and my band on our toes. They never know what I'm going to say or what I'm going to do next, so they stay interested in the show and don't loose concentration—because if they do, they're lost. We all have fun and hopefully it will become contagious to the crowd and they'll have fun along with us."

—NEAL McCOY

FRESH PEACH COBBLER

¼ cup + 2 tbsp. butter
   or margarine
2 cups sugar, divided
¾ cup all-purpose flour
2 tsp. baking powder
   dash of salt
¾ cup milk
2 cups peaches, sliced

- Melt butter in a 2-quart baking dish. Combine 1 cup sugar, flour, baking powder, and salt; add milk, and stir until mixed. Pour batter over butter in baking dish, but do not stir.
- Combine peaches and remaining 1 cup sugar; spoon over the batter. Do not stir. Bake at 350 degrees for 1 hour.

YIELDS 6–8 SERVINGS.

Prepared for T. Graham Brown.

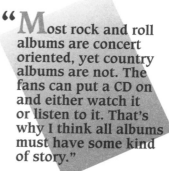

"**M**ost rock and roll albums are concert oriented, yet country albums are not. The fans can put a CD on and either watch it or listen to it. That's why I think all albums must have some kind of story."

—REX ALLEN, JR.

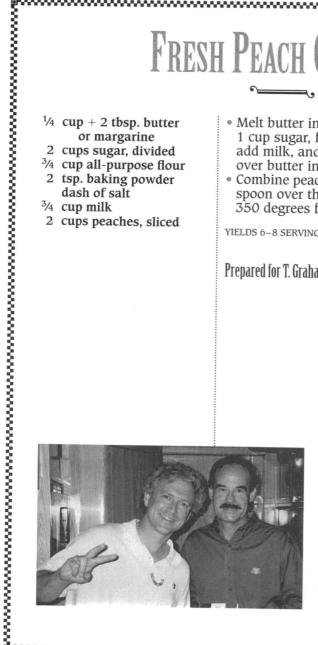

ALL AMERICAN APPLE PIE

PASTRY

2 cups all-purpose flour
1 tsp. salt
2/3 cup shortening or lard
6–7 tbsp. cold water

- In medium mixing bowl, stir together flour and salt. Cut in shortening or lard till pieces are the size of small peas. Sprinkle 1 tablespoon water over part of mixture; gently toss with a fork. Push to side of bowl. Repeat until all is moistened.
- Form dough into 2 balls. On lightly floured surface, flatten one ball of dough with hands. Roll dough from center to edge, forming a circle about 12 inches in diameter.
- Ease pastry into pie plate, being careful to avoid stretching pastry. Trim pastry even with rim of pie plate. For top crust, roll out second ball of dough. Place apple filling in pie shell. Top with pastry for top crust. Cut slits for escape of steam. Trim top crust ½ inch beyond edge of pie plate. Fold extra pastry under bottom crust; flute edge.
- To prevent over browning, cover edge of pie with foil. Bake in 375 degree oven for 25 minutes. Remove foil; bake for 20 to 25 minutes more or till crust is golden. Cool pie on rack.

"**I** like to entertain the audience by reaching out and joking with them. I like to make them feel close. I like to think of them as 50 thousand friends out there."

—MARK WILLS

FILLING

6 cups cooking apples, thinly sliced
1 tbsp. lemon juice
1 cup sugar
2 tbsp. all-purpose flour
1 tsp. ground cinnamon
dash ground nutmeg
1 tbsp. butter

- Sprinkle apples with lemon juice. In mixing bowl, combine sugar, flour, cinnamon, and nutmeg. Add sugar mixture to the sliced apples; toss to mix. Fill pastry lined pie plate with apple mixture; dot with butter.

Prepared for Pam Tillis.

PEACH PIE

PASTRY

2 egg whites, room
   temperature
pinch salt
1/8 tsp. cream of tartar
1/2 cup sugar
1/2 cup pecans, chopped
1/2 tsp. vanilla extract

• Beat egg whites slightly. Add salt and cream of tartar. Beat until soft peaks form, gradually adding sugar, 2 tablespoons at a time. Fold in nuts and vanilla extract. Pour into buttered 9-inch pie pan, spreading evenly over bottom and sides. Place in cold oven. Bake 40 minutes at 300 degrees, or until lightly browned. This may be made the day before serving. Refrigerate.

FILLING

1 pkg. (3 oz.) cream
   cheese
1/2 cup powdered sugar
1/2 tsp. almond extract
1 container (9 oz.)
   non-dairy whipped
   topping
1 can (16 oz.) peach
   slices, drained

• In bowl of electric mixer, blend cream cheese, sugar, and almond extract; add whipped topping. Fold in peach slices. Pour into pie shell and chill.

YIELDS 1 (9-INCH) PIE.

Prepared for Tracy Byrd.

"I try to record songs that have different messages—hopefully things I stand for—and sometimes, they're even funny."

—GARTH BROOKS

STRAWBERRY CAKE

1 box white cake mix
½ cup cooking oil
1 pkg. strawberry jello
4 eggs
½ cup water
½ cup fresh or frozen
    strawberries

- Grease and flour two 9-inch cake pans.
- Combine all ingredients in bowl. Beat until smooth and pour into pans.
- Bake at 350 degrees for 30 minutes. After cakes cool, frost with the following recipe.

FROSTING/FILLING

- Cream 1 stick margarine, 1 box powdered sugar, and ½ cup fresh or frozen strawberries until smooth enough to spread.

Prepared for Ronnie McDowell.

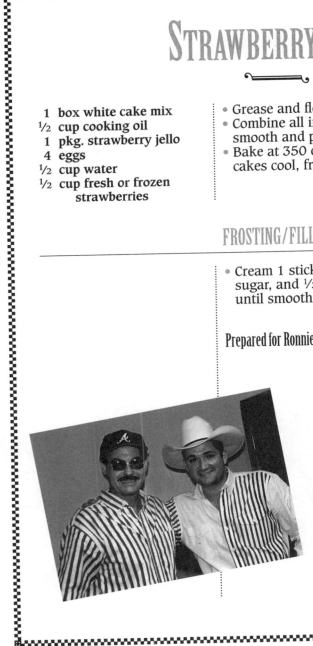

"I think country music sounds more human, less programmed and less synthesized than any other music."

—LIONEL CARTWRIGHT

LEMON JELLO CAKE

1 box lemon cake mix
4 eggs
1 pkg. lemon jello
¾ cup Crisco oil
¾ cup water

- Mix and beat 4 minutes. Bake in 9×13 inch pan at 350 degrees for 30–35 minutes.

FROSTING

1½ cup powdered sugar
juice of 2 lemons

- Mix two ingredients and spread on top of cake in pan as soon as it comes out of oven.

Prepared for Bryan White.

"Country music is life. It is a life experience; it has been, it is now, and always will be."

—REX ALLEN, JR.

CANDY ORANGE SLICE CAKE

1½ cups sugar
1 cup margarine
   or butter
4 eggs
1 can (3½ oz.) Angel
   Flake coconut
1 lb. orange slice candy
8 oz. pitted dates
2 cups pecans
1 tsp. soda mixed
   in buttermilk
½ cup buttermilk
2 cups plain flour

- Chop or cut candy, dates, and nuts into small pieces. Melt margarine or butter and pour over the chopped ingredients. Mix sugar, eggs, flour, and buttermilk together and pour over melted margarine and other ingredients. Add angel flake coconut, blending all together.
- Bake in greased and floured tube pan for 2 hours at 300 degrees.

Prepared for the Bellamy Brothers.

"**I** think country music makes you aware that the common man is great and it glorifies that, as opposed to glorifying the singer. I think that's what makes country music great."

—LIONEL CARTWRIGHT

Orange Slice Cake

3½ cup flour, sifted
½ tsp. salt
½ tsp. soda*
1 lb. orange slice candy, chopped
1 pkg. (1 lb.) pitted dates, chopped
2 cups walnuts or (16 oz.) pecans, chopped
1 can (3½ oz.) flaked coconut
1 cup margarine
1 cups sugar
4 eggs
1 tsp. baking soda
½ cup buttermilk
1 tsp. orange rind, grated (optional)
   *Omit if using self-rising flour.

- Cream margarine and sugar well. Add eggs 1 at a time, alternately with flour. Add soda to buttermilk and pour in mixture. Sprinkle dates, nuts, and candy with flour until coated and add to mixture. Add coconut to batter.
- Pour into pan which has been greased and lined with wax paper.
- Bake at 300 degrees for 1½–1¾ hours. Place pan of water under rack to keep cake moist.

> **"I** think music can be a great communication tool; it can be a healing tool for people. It can bring people together."
>
> —Lionel Cartwright

GLAZE

1 cup orange juice
1–2 cups powdered sugar

- Combine ingredients and mix well. Pour over warm cake. Chill overnight before removing from pan.

VARIATION:
This caterer sometimes bakes her cake at 225 degrees for 3 hours, and adds grated orange rind to the glaze.

Prepared for Billy Dean.

Lazy Dazy Oatmeal Cake

1¼ cup boiling water
1 cup quick-cooking oats
½ cup margarine
1 cup brown sugar, packed
1 cup white sugar
2 eggs
1½ cup flour, sifted
1 tsp. soda
½ tsp. salt
¼ tsp. nutmeg
¾ tsp. cinnamon
1 tsp. vanilla

- Pour boiling water over oats. Mix well; set aside. Cream butter and sugars thoroughly, beat in eggs. Stir in soaked oatmeal. Sift together flour and other dry ingredients. Add to mixture.
- Bake at 350 degrees for 35-50 minutes in a 7×11 inch baking pan that has been greased and floured.

BROILED TOPPING

⅓ cup margarine
¾ cup brown sugar
¼ cup Half & Half
⅓ cup pecans, chopped
1 cup Angel Flake coconut

- Melt margarine and mix with sugar and cream until smooth. Add pecans and coconut. Spread on hot cake and broil for a few minutes.

Prepared for Dottie West.

"**S**ometimes, when things get tough for me, I like to remember a statement that I once heard Bob Dylan say, 'God will never let you get in so deep that he and you can't get out.' When I am troubled there are two things that I reach for—that's the Bible and music."

—Garth Brooks

FRESH APPLE CAKE

3 cups plain flour
1½ tsp. baking soda
½ tsp. salt
1 tsp. cinnamon
2 cups sugar
2 eggs
1¼ cup salad oil
3½ cups apples, chopped
1½ cups nuts, chopped
2 tsp. vanilla

- Sift together twice flour, soda, salt, and cinnamon. Beat eggs and sugar until creamy. Add oil and vanilla. Beat until smooth. Add sifted flour mixture to form stiff dough. Stir in apples and nuts.
- Pour into greased and floured tube pan. Bake at 350 degrees for 1 hour.

Prepared for Leroy Parnell.

"**A** lot of times when I've got a problem I handle it the same way Andy did on the Andy Griffith TV show. People used to say that I was just like him."

—DANNY SHIRLEY

APPLE CAKE

1½ cup Wesson oil
2 cups sugar
3 lg. eggs
3 cups sifted cake flour
1 tsp. soda
1 tsp. salt
1½ cup nuts, chopped
1 tsp. vanilla
3 cups raw apples, sliced

• Mix in order given and pour in large greased pan. Bake at 325 degrees for 1 hour. Leave cake in pan and cover with glaze.

GLAZE

1 cup light brown sugar
1 stick margarine
¼ cup cream
1 tsp. vanilla

• Combine all ingredients in a sauce pan and cook for 2½ minutes, stirring constantly. Spoon over cake while both are still warm.

Prepared for James Bonamy.

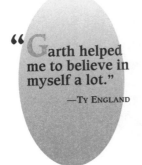

"Garth helped me to believe in myself a lot."
—Ty England

APPLESAUCE CAKE

2½ cups flour, sifted
1¾ cups sugar
¼ tsp. baking powder
1½ tsp. salt
1 tsp. cloves
1½ tsp. baking soda
½ cup shortening
1 can (15 oz.)
   applesauce
3 eggs
1 cup seedless raisins,
   chopped
1 cup walnuts, finely
   chopped
½ tsp. nutmeg

- Preheat oven to 350 degrees. Grease well and flour a 13×9×2 inch pan.
- Sift flour, sugar, baking powder, baking soda, salt, and spices into a large bowl. Add shortening and applesauce. Beat 1 minute at low speed to combine. At medium speed beat 2 minutes, constantly cleaning side of bowl with rubber scraper and guiding batter into beaters. Add eggs and beat 2 minutes. Combine raisins and walnuts. Add to batter, pour batter into prepared pan.
- Bake 45 minutes, cool and frost as desired.

Prepared for Lionel Cartwright.

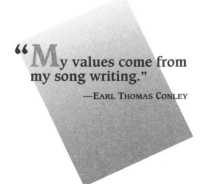

"My values come from my song writing."
—EARL THOMAS CONLEY

CARROT CAKE #1

2 cups carrots, grated
1 cup nuts, chopped
1 cup apples, coarsely chopped
1 cup crushed pineapple, well-drained
1 tsp. vanilla
3 cups plain flour
2 cups sugar
1½ tsp. baking powder
1 tsp. soda
1 tsp. salt
1½ cup salad oil
3 eggs, lightly beaten

- Mix together carrots, nuts, apples, pineapple, and vanilla.
- Mix together all dry ingredients—flour, sugar, baking powder, soda, and salt. Add salad oil and eggs to flour mixture. Stir in fruit mixture.
- Bake 1 hour in greased and floured 9×13 inch pan at 350 degrees.

Prepared for Kitty Wells.

"It makes me very uncomfortable to be called a role model. But if someone is going to listen to what I say, then I want to impress upon them that God exists, your best friends are your family, and that there's really nothing you can't do. If success can happen to me, it can happen to anybody."

—GARTH BROOKS

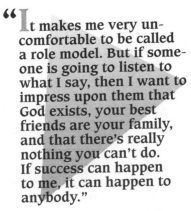

CARROT CAKE #2

3 eggs
2 cups sugar
1¼ cups vegetable oil
3 cups all-purpose flour
2 tsp. soda
1 tsp. salt
2 tsp. ground cinnamon
1½ cups carrots, grated
1 cup pecans, chopped
1 can (20 oz.) crushed pineapple, well drained
2 tsp. vanilla extract

- Combine eggs, sugar, and oil in a large mixing bowl; then beat well.
- Combine flour, soda, salt, and cinnamon; add to sugar mixture, and beat well. Stir in carrots, pecans, pineapple, and vanilla.
- Pour into a greased and floured 10-inch tube pan. Bake at 350 degrees for 1 hour and 15 minutes or until wooden pick inserted in center comes out clean. Cool in pan 10 to 15 minutes; remove from pan, and let cool completely.

Prepared for Daron Norwood.

"**I** don't want anybody to paint a better picture of me that what I truly am."
—GARTH BROOKS

PINEAPPLE SOUR CREAM CAKE

2 cups sour cream
2 cups sugar
2 pkg. (6 oz.) frozen
    coconut
2 cans (8¼ oz.) crushed
    pineapple, drained
1 box yellow cake mix

- Combine sour cream, sugar, coconut, and 1 can crushed pineapple in a bowl. Refrigerate overnight.
- Prepare cake mix according to package directions. Stir in other can of pineapple. Pour in greased 9×13 inch pan and bake according to box directions.
- After cooling, spread sour cream mixture evenly over cake. Keep refrigerated.

Prepared for Doug Supernaw.

"The good Lord gave me my talent. As long as people want to hear me, that's how long I will sing. If you are used as a tool instead of a weapon, you can do a lot of good."

—DARRELL MCCALL

OLD-FASHIONED, HOMEMADE COCONUT CAKE

2 cups sifted self-rising
  flour
1¼ cups sugar
½ cup shortening (Crisco)
¾ cup milk
3 eggs
1 tsp. vanilla

- Heat oven to 350 degrees. Grease three 9-inch pans and dust with flour.
- Sift together flour and sugar. Add shortening and slightly over ½ of the milk. Blend, then beat 2 minutes at medium speed. Add remaining milk, eggs, and vanilla. Blend, then beat 2 minutes at high speed.
- Pour batter into pans and bake 23 to 30 minutes. Let cake cool in pans. While cake is cooling, grate coconut and save juice. Place juice and grated coconut in refrigerator until ready to make icing.

ICING

2½ cups sugar
1¼ cup milk
1 tsp. vanilla
1 stick butter
  grated coconut

- Cook milk and sugar until it ropes from the spoon. Remove from heat and add butter and vanilla. Add grated coconut, saving small portion to sprinkle on top.
- As you stack your cake layers, poke holes in the layers and spread the coconut juice over the layers. Add the icing. The icing will not spread on the sides of the cake. Cake is better if you let it set overnight before serving.

Prepared for Blackhawk.

"**M**usic is like a sword. You can use it to kill or use it to fight for the good in the world. Everyday I pick it up and say 'God, hold on to me because here we go again.'"

—GARTH BROOKS

EASY POUND CAKE #1

1	lb. powdered sugar
6	eggs
3¼	cups plain flour
1	tsp. vanilla
¾	lb. margarine

- Cream sugar and margarine. Add eggs one at a time; add flour gradually, then add vanilla.
- Bake at 300 degrees for approximately 1 hour in a pan which has been greased and floured.

Prepared for Garth Brooks.

"**I**f you can stick to your own path, all else will be right. If you are right with yourself, you can truly live—like the Cherokee call it—in the seventh direction. You can handle anything that comes. You can allow things to flow through you or around you."

—HAL KETCHUM

EASY POUND CAKE #2

1 cup Crisco
2 cups sugar
1 tsp. lemon flavoring
2 cups plain flour
6 eggs

- Cream Crisco and sugar until fluffy. Add eggs one at a time; blend flour, then flavoring.
- Place in cold oven. Set oven 350 degrees, bake 60–70 minutes.

Prepared for Lari White.

"The thing about music is that you can make people laugh or make them cry. If it doesn't move people emotionally one way or another, then the song may not be the one you should be doing. Country music songs contain bits and pieces of someone's life."

— MARTY RAYBON

COLD OVEN POUND CAKE

2 sticks butter
½ cup shortening
3 cups sugar
5 eggs
3 cups flour
½ tsp. salt
1 cup evaporated milk
1 tsp. lemon flavoring
2 tsp. vanilla flavoring
½ tsp. baking powder

- Cream butter and shortening to consistency of mayonnaise; gradually add sugar and cream until very fluffy. Beat in eggs one at a time. Add sifted flour and salt alternately with milk; mix well. Add flavorings and blend well.
- Pour into greased tube pan. Sprinkle baking powder over batter; cut into batter with a knife.
- Place pan in a cold oven. Set oven at 350 degrees and bake 1 hour and 30 minutes or until done.

Prepared for Mel McDaniel.

"**M**usic permeated my life. It just swept me up whether I liked it or not."

—JOHN HARTFORD

SOUR CREAM POUND CAKE

3 cups granulated sugar
3 cups plain flour
1 cup Crisco
1 cup sour cream
pinch salt
¼ tsp. soda
6 eggs
1 tsp. vanilla flavoring
1 tsp. lemon flavoring

- Take a big bowl and mix the above ingredients in the order shown.
- Beat four minutes. Bake in greased and floured tube pan 1½ hours at 300 degrees.

FILLING

½ stick margarine, melted
½ box powdered sugar
2 tbsp. sweet milk
1 tsp. vanilla flavoring
1 tsp. lemon flavoring

- Combine and put on hot cake.

Prepared for Charlie Daniels.

"The music has got to reach and touch somebody. One person may take a song entirely differently from the person sitting next to them. There should always be more than one way to interpret a song."

—MARTY RAYBON

Coconut Pound Cake #1

1½ cups Crisco
2½ cups sugar
5 eggs
1 cup milk
3 cups plain flour
¼ tsp. salt
1 tbsp. coconut
flavoring
1 cup coconut

- Beat Crisco and sugar for 10 minutes. Add eggs, one at a time. Mix milk, flour, and salt alternately. Add flavoring. Add coconut.
- Pour in greased tube pan. Bake at 350 degrees for 1 hour and 30 minutes.

Prepared for Hal Ketchum.

"I kinda write for the times because that's what is happening now and I see things that I can relate to. I really relate to people because I was a blue-collar laborer for so long."

—Joe Diffie

Coconut Pound Cake # 2

1 cup shortening
¾ stick butter
2¾ cups sugar
6 eggs
1 cup milk with
    8–10 drops yellow
    food coloring
1 tsp. vanilla and
    ½ tsp. butter
    flavoring in milk
3 cups cake flour
1½ tsp. salt
1 tsp. baking powder
1½ cup coconut

- Cream shortening, butter, and sugar until light. Add eggs one at a time and beat.
- Sift together flour, salt, and baking powder. Sift twice. Add the shortening mixture alternately with milk. Add coconut and bake in bundt pan at 325 degrees for 1 hour 15 minutes.

SAUCE

1 cup sugar
½ cup water
1 tsp. coconut flavoring
¼ cup white corn syrup

- Boil together five minutes. Pour over cake in pan while hot. Let cool in pan.

Prepared for Holly Dunn.

"Country music is a little bit of the old and a little bit of the new. The format is not really changing. Country will never go pop. It's the language and music of blue collar America. A lot of people who grew up in the sixties and seventies are now running the record labels and writing the songs. They have a respect for the traditional side of country music but they have the fire and desire to make some changes. I think that's healthy."

—DAVE GIBSON

FRESH COCONUT CAKE

1½ cups coconut, freshly grated

3 cups cake flour (sift before measuring)
RESIFT BAKING POWDER & SALT WITH SIFTED FLOUR

3 tsp. double-acting baking powder

½ tsp. salt

1½ cups sugar, sifted

¾ cup butter

3 eggs, separated

¾ cup coconut milk

½ tsp. vanilla

- Preheat oven to 350 degrees.
- Have all ingredients at about 75 degrees. Have ready 1½ cups freshly grated coconut.
- Cream butter and add the sifted sugar gradually and continue creaming until these ingredients are very light. Beat in 3 beaten egg yolks.
- Add the sifted flour mixture in 3 parts to butter mixture, alternating with the coconut milk and vanilla. Stir the batter until smooth after each addition. Then add ¾ cup of the grated coconut.
- Whip until stiff 3 egg whites. Fold the egg whites gently into the batter. Bake in greased layer pans for about 25 minutes. Cool completely and remove from pans.

SEA-FOAM ICING

2 beaten egg whites

1½ cups sugar

5 tbsp. cold water

¼ tsp. cream of tartar

1½ tsp. light corn syrup

- Place all 5 ingredients in the top of a double boiler and beat until thoroughly blended.
- Place the blended ingredients over rapidly boiling water. Beat them constantly with medium speed mixer for 8 minutes. Remove icing from heat. Add 1 teaspoon vanilla. Continue beating until the icing is the right consistency to be spread.
- To serve, fill strawberry or raspberry jelly between the layers. Cover the top and sides of cake with sea-foam icing.

Prepared for Loretta Lynn.

COCONUT PECAN POUND CAKE

2 sticks butter
⅓ cup shortening (Crisco)
3 cups sugar
5 eggs
3 cups plain cake flour
1 cup milk
1 tsp. baking powder
1 tsp. coconut flavoring
1 pkg. (7 oz.) Angel
   Flake coconut
1½ cups pecans, chopped

- Cream butter, shortening, and sugar. Add eggs and remaining ingredients.
- Pour into greased, floured 10-inch tube pan. Bake at 325 degrees for 1½ hours.

Prepared for Marty Robbins.

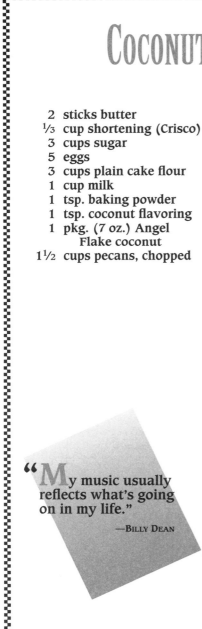

"**M**y music usually reflects what's going on in my life."

—BILLY DEAN

CREAM CHEESE POUND CAKE

3	sticks cinnamon
8	oz. cream cheese
3	cups sugar
	dash of salt
1½	tsp. vanilla
6	eggs
3	cups flour, sifted

- Cream together margarine, cream cheese, and sugar. Add a dash of salt and vanilla. Beat until fluffy. Add eggs, one at a time beating after each. Stir in sifted flour.
- Pour into a greased and floured 10-inch tube pan. Bake at 300 degrees for 1½ hours or until toothpick comes out clean.

Prepared for Gene Watson.

"**I**n country music today, record labels and producers have figured out a formula for success. They can take an act that has no fan base in the market place, select great songs that are pigeonholed for a specific market, and then shoot a video. This 'sound with an attitude' really sells."

—PAUL OVERSTREET

MAMA'S POUND CAKE #1

½ cup Crisco
2 sticks margarine
6 eggs
3 cups plain flour
3 cups sugar
½ tsp. baking powder
2 tsp. vanilla
¼ tsp. salt
1¼ cup sweet milk

- Cream Crisco, margarine, and sugar together. Add eggs, beating after each one.
- Sift flour, salt, and baking powder together. Alternate adding flour mixture and milk. Add vanilla last.
- Bake at 350 degrees for 1 hour. Test with toothpick for doneness.

SUGGESTION:
I only use 1 teaspoon vanilla, but I add 1 teaspoon of lemon and 1 teaspoon of coconut flavoring. This makes for a delicious flavor.

Prepared for Rex Allen Jr.

" **Y**ou have to change to grow. There is nothing new under the sun. It's all been done before. It just comes back in a new form."

—DAVE GIBSON

Mama's Pound Cake #2

1 cup Crisco (Buttery)
2 cups sugar
2 cups plain flour
¼ tsp. baking powder
6 eggs

- Cream Crisco, add sugar and continue to mix until smooth.
- Sift flour and baking powder together. Add to the shortening-sugar mixture alternately with the eggs.
- Bake at 350 degrees for 1 hour. Test with toothpick for doneness. Turn out on rack. Do not leave turned on top—it will sweat and ruin the crunchy top.

Prepared for Tom Wopat.

"When you grow, you keep your roots, you keep your foundation. You expand but not really change."

—BLUE MILLER

BROWN SUGAR POUND CAKE

1 cup butter
½ cup shortening
1 pkg. (16 oz.) brown
    sugar
½ cup sugar
5 lg. eggs
½ tsp. baking powder
3 cups all-purpose flour
1 cup milk
2 tbsp. vanilla extract
1 cup pecans, chopped

- Cream butter and shortening in a large mixing bowl; gradually add sugar, beating until light and fluffy. Add eggs, one at a time, beating well after each addition.
- Combine baking powder and flour; add to creamed mixture alternately with milk beginning and ending with flour, and beating well after each addition. Stir in vanilla and pecans.
- Pour batter into greased and floured 10-inch tube pan. Bake at 350 for 1 hour and 10 minutes or until a wooden pick inserted in center comes out clean. Cool in pan 10 minutes; invert on wire rack to cool completely.

CREAM CHEESE FROSTING

½ cup butter
1 pkg. (8 oz.) cream
    cheese, softened
2 tsp. vanilla extract
1 pkg. (16 oz.) brown
    sugar

- Combine all ingredients, mixing until smooth.

Prepared for George Strait.

"Country music has always been alive and it'll never die, but it has expanded so much, and so many different people have been exposed to it."

—JOHNNY LEE

EASY POUND CAKE

1 box Duncan Hines
 butter cake mix
5 eggs
1 cup sour cream
¼ cup sugar
½ cup Wesson oil*

*Be sure it is Wesson oil.

• Mix and bake at 325 for 1 hour.

Prepared for Ken Mellons.

"I think that country music is healthy in that it is encompassing so many influences. I think involved in that whole spectrum is this traditionalism that pervades the entire industry."

—RADNEY FOSTER

POUND CAKE WITH FRUIT SAUCE

1 yellow cake mix
⅔ cup oil
⅔ cup water
1 box instant vanilla
    Jello pudding
4 eggs

- Mix above ingredients sequentially as shown, adding eggs one at a time.
- Bake at 325 degrees for 55 to 60 minutes in greased and floured 10-inch tube pan.

FRUIT SAUCE

1 cup cold milk
1 tbsp. orange juice
1 lg. pkg. yellow instant
    pudding mix
1 cup Cool Whip
1 sm. carton sour cream

- Mix ingredients until smooth and add fruit. Spoon mixture over cake as served.

1 can (11 oz.) mandarin oranges
    blueberries
    strawberries
    kiwi
    pineapple
    green grapes, cut in halves

Prepared for Ronnie Milsap.

"I do what I do, everybody else does what they do, and the music goes where it was going to go anyway."

—JOHN HARTFORD

Red Velvet Cake #1

1½ cups sugar
2 eggs
2½ cups cake flour
1½ cups cooking oil
1 cup buttermilk
1 tsp. vanilla flavoring
1 tsp. soda
1 tsp. vinegar
1 oz. red cake coloring

- Beat eggs, add sugar, cooking oil, and vinegar.
- Sift cake flour and soda together. Add flour to mixture. Add milk to mixture slowly. Add flavoring and cake coloring.
- Bake in 3 greased and floured 9-inch cake pans at 350 degrees for 25 minutes.

FILLING

1 box powdered sugar
1 8 oz. cream cheese
1 stick butter

- Place cream cheese and butter over low heat. Let melt and add powdered sugar. Add pecans and flavoring if desired.

Prepared for Don Williams.

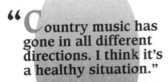

"Country music has gone in all different directions. I think it's a healthy situation."

—Leroy Van Dyke

RED VELVET CAKE #2

2½ cups cake flour
2 cups sugar
4 eggs
1 tsp. salt
1 tsp. vanilla
1 bottle red food
    coloring
1 cup buttermilk
2 sticks butter
½ cup Wesson oil
1 tsp. soda
1 tsp. vinegar
2 tsp. cocoa

- Cream sugar with oil and butter; add eggs and beat well. Add vanilla.
- Mix cocoa and good coloring in a separate bowl. Add vinegar and mix well.
- Combine all of second mixture with the sugar-butter.
- Sift flour, soda, and salt together. Add dry ingredients alternately with buttermilk to the sugar-butter mixture.
- Bake at 350 degrees for 25 minutes. Makes 3 layers.

ICING FOR RED VELVET CAKE

1 stick margarine
1 box 4X powdered sugar
1 tsp. vanilla
1 cup pecans, chopped
1 pkg. (8 oz.) cream cheese

- Mix well and spread icing on cooled layers of cake.

Prepared for Dolly Parton.

"There's not too many new trails to blaze in music."

—JEFF HANNAH

Easy Cup Cakes

1   cup granulated sugar
⅓   cup shortening
1¾ cups cake flour, sifted
2   eggs, well beaten
1½ tsp. baking powder
½   cup milk
1   tsp. vanilla

- Sift flour and baking powder together.
- Cream shortening and sugar. Add eggs, then flour, alternating with small amounts of milk. Beat until smooth. Add flavoring.
- Pour into greased cup cake pans, filling each space a little more than half full. Bake in moderate oven 350–375 degrees about 20 minutes. Ice with butter cream frosting.

Prepared for Johnny Lee.

"I think that country music is the most creative music around because there are so many people involved in the business today. That makes it very creative. I think that more than anything we need to let the public define country music and not a group of record executives."

—Rex Allen, Jr.

CRUNCHY NUT MUFFINS

1½ cups unbleached
    all-purpose flour
½ cup sugar
¼ cup cornmeal
¼ cup wheat germ
2 tbsp. baking powder
½ tsp. salt
1½ cups unprocessed bran
½ cup granola
2 cups buttermilk
1½ tbsp. crunchy peanut
    butter
2½ tbsp. vegetable oil
2 eggs, beaten

- Combine the first 6 ingredients in a large mixing bowl; set mixture aside.
- Combine bran, granola, and buttermilk; mix well, and soak 5 minutes. Add peanut butter, vegetable oil, and eggs, mixing well.
- Make a well in center of dry ingredients; pour in liquid ingredients. Stir just until moistened.
- Fill greased muffin pans two-thirds full. Bake at 400 degrees for 25 minutes. Remove from pan immediately.

YIELDS ABOUT 2 DOZEN MUFFINS.

Prepared for Hal Ketchum.

"It's an exciting time to be in country music. It's like Vince Gill said, 'Country music is not changing, it's just expanding.'"

—BLUE MILLER

LEMON SPONGE CUPS

1   cup sugar
2   tbsp. butter
3   eggs
1½ cups milk
5   tbsp. lemon juice
    rind of 1 lemon, grated
4   tbsp. flour
    pinch of salt

- Cream butter. Add sugar, flour, salt, lemon juice, and grated rind. Stir in beaten egg yolks mixed with milk. Fold in stiffly beaten egg whites.
- Pour into glass custard cups. Set the cups in a pan of water and bake about 45 minutes at 350 degrees. When done each cup will contain custard at the bottom and sponge cake on top.

Prepared for Bryan White.

"To me, country people will accept anything that's genuine, and that they can understand and relate to. What's good about country music fans is that they're not fickle. If you prove to them that you're for real, they will stick with you."

—HOWARD BELLAMY

DOUBLE FUDGE BROWNIES

1½ cups flour, unsifted
½ tsp. baking soda
½ tsp. salt
⅔ cup butter
1½ cups sugar
¼ cup water
1 pkg. (12 oz.) Nestle Semi-Sweet Real Chocolate Morsels
2 tsp. vanilla extract
4 eggs
1 cup nuts, chopped

- Preheat oven to 325 degrees.
- In small bowl, combine flour, baking soda, and salt; set aside.
- In small saucepan, combine butter, sugar, and water; bring just to a boil. Remove from heat. Add Nestle Semi-Sweet Chocolate Morsels and vanilla extract; stir until morsels melt and mixture is smooth. Transfer to large bowl.
- Add eggs, one at a time, beating well after each addition. Gradually blend in flour mixture. Stir in nuts.
- Spread into greased 13×9×2 inch baking pan. Bake at 325 degrees for 50 minutes. Cool and cut into 1½-inch squares.

YIELDS 2 DOZEN 2-INCH SQUARES.

Prepared for Lee Greenwood.

"**I** think sooner or later people begin to long for realism when they haven't had it for a while. The hype, the clothes, the certain look that sells records—all that goes away. Real talent is always there—it doesn't go away."

—PAUL OVERSTREET

BUTTER PECAN COOKIES

2 cups all-purpose flour
½ tsp. salt
1 cup butter, softened
2 tbsp. sugar
¼ cup light molasses
2 cups pecans, finely chopped
powdered sugar

- Combine flour and salt; set aside.
- Cream butter and sugar in a large mixing bowl until light and fluffy. Add molasses; mix until well blended. Gradually add flour mixture to butter mixture; mix well. Stir pecans into dough.
- Roll dough into 1-inch balls; place about 2 inches apart on ungreased cookie sheets. Bake at 350 degrees for 15 to 18 minutes.
- Dust or roll warm cookies in powdered sugar.

YIELDS ABOUT 5 DOZEN COOKIES.

Prepared for Paul Overstreet.

"**I**'m not going to change the way I feel or anything I'm going to do just because the business may not always favor me. I will continue to do country music and I will do it from the heart."

—DARYLE SINGLETARY

MOLASSES SUGAR COOKIES

¾ cup shortening
1 cup sugar
¼ cup molasses
1 egg, beaten
2¼ cups all-purpose flour
2 tsp. soda
½ tsp. salt
½ tsp. ground gloves
1 tsp. ground ginger
1 tsp. ground cinnamon
   sugar

- Melt shortening and cool. Add 1 cup sugar, molasses, and egg; mix well.
- Combine flour, soda, salt, and spices; add to sugar mixture, mixing until blended.
- Shape dough into 1-inch balls; roll in sugar. Place 2 inches apart on greased cookie sheets; bake at 375 degrees for 8 minutes or until done.

YIELDS ABOUT 4 DOZEN.

Prepared for Ernest Tubb.

"There's always going to be those die-hard country music fans out there that don't follow the fads. They are always going to need their country music and they're always going to need someone to give it to them. As long as that holds true, I'm not going to worry."

—TRACE ATKINS

BACKSTAGE CREAM CHEESE COFFEE CAKE

PASTRY

3 oz. cream cheese
¼ cup margarine
2¼ cups Bisquick
½ cup milk

- Preheat oven to 400 degrees.
- Cut 3 ounces cream cheese and margarine into Bisquick. Stir in milk. Knead. Roll into rectangle 9×12 inches. Place on lightly greased baking sheet.

FILLING

8 oz. cream cheese
½ cup sugar
¼ tsp. vanilla

- Beat filling ingredients and spread down center of dough. Make cuts 2½ inches long at 1 inch intervals. Fold over filling.
- Bake 20 minutes. Cool 10 minutes.

GLAZE

¾ cup powdered sugar
1 tbsp. warm water
¼ tsp. vanilla

- Mix glaze ingredients and drizzle.

OPTIONAL:
Chopped nuts on top.

Prepared for backstage party for John Denver.

"**I** grew up with a lot of country music. But even more than that, I grew up with music."

—EDDIE RABBITT

MINNIE'S TEA CAKES

4 cups plain flour
1 cup butter
2 eggs
⅓ cup buttermilk
1 tsp. vanilla
1 tsp. baking powder
1 cup sugar, heaping
1 tsp. soda
½ tsp. salt

- Mix all dry ingredients well, then add eggs, milk, and vanilla. Continue stirring until well mixed.
- Roll out dough and cut into desired shapes and bake.

Prepared for Minnie Pearl.

"Country music is what I am. That's what I grew up on. That's what I do."

—TRACE ATKINS

Peanut Butter Cream Candy

2 cups white sugar
1½ cups cold water
1 tbsp. vanilla flavoring
2 cups peanut butter
oatmeal as needed

• Cook until a drop from spoon forms ball in cold water. Remove from heat. Add vanilla and peanut butter. Mix until no lumps are left. Then add enough oatmeal to thicken. Pour on cookie sheet. After candy is cooled, cut into pieces.

Prepared for Leroy Van Dyke.

"**S**ometimes country music is accused of having too many ditties and bubble gum kind of things. Some of the female singers are releasing quality music right now. It contains a lot of messages for the youth. For example, you may get hurt bad, but you can make it through it. You may be lonely, but you're not alone. There are a lot of values and morals you have to stick with. The family is still very important. There's a lot of strength in country music."

—Katy Hass

CREAMY PEACH FREEZE

1 pkg. (1¼ oz.) whipped
   topping mix
1 can (16 oz.) sliced
   peaches, drained

- Prepare whipped topping mix according to package directions. Combine whipped topping and peaches in container of electric blender; process until smooth. Spoon into 4 serving dishes; freeze 2 to 3 hours or until firm.
- Remove from freezer 5 minutes before serving.

YIELDS 4 SERVINGS.

Prepared for Mark Collie.

" Country music is popular all over the world because it has heart—it has meaning—more than any other music in the industry."

—GAYLE STRICKLAND

Part Seven

BREADS

POP'S CORN BREAD DRESSING

½ cup butter, melted
1 cup onions, chopped
1 cup celery, chopped
1 cup bread crumbs
6 cups corn bread, crumbled
1 cup saltine cracker crumbs
1½ cups cooked grits
3 cups broth
3 eggs, beaten
½ tsp. salt
½ tsp. black pepper
1 tsp. poultry seasoning

- Preheat oven to 450 degrees.
- In a large skillet over medium heat, heat butter and sauté onions and celery until soft, about 10 minutes.
- In a large bowl, combine bread crumbs, corn bread, cracker crumbs, grits, broth, and eggs. Add cooked vegetables, salt, pepper, and poultry seasoning. Mix well.
- Pour into a 2½-quart baking dish and bake until brown and firm, about 30 to 40 minutes.

YIELDS 6 SERVINGS.

Prepared for Ty England.

"**C**ountry music is popular all over the world because it has heart—it has meaning—more than any other music in the industry."

—GAYLE STRICKLAND

SOUTHERN CORN BREAD

2 cups corn meal (white
     or yellow)
2 tsp. Calumet Baking
     Powder
1 tsp. soda
1½ tsp. salt
2 cups sour milk
     or buttermilk
2 eggs, unbeaten
⅓ cup shortening, melted

- Mix together corn meal, baking powder, soda, and salt.
- Add sour milk, eggs, and shortening. Mix well.
- Turn into well-greased 13×9×1 inch pan and bake in hot oven at 425 degrees for 35 minutes. Or turn into well-greased 9×9×2 inch pan and bake in hot oven at 425 degrees for 45 minutes. The pan must be shallow for good browning.

NOTE:
For corn sticks, turn the corn bread batter into hot greased iron corn stick pans and bake in hot oven at 450 degrees for 20 minutes.

YIELDS 20 CORN STICKS.

Prepared for Patty Lovelace.

"**W**hen I wrote 'God Bless the USA,' I saw America in pieces and in dire need of healing. I really wanted to write this song to tie the nation together. The timing was sort of guided by the Lord's hand. I hope that my music makes people smile, and feel the spirit of America."

—LEE GREENWOOD

OLD FASHIONED SPOON BREAD

1 cup cornmeal
½ tsp. salt
2 tbsp. butter
4 eggs, beaten
1 cup milk

- Stir cornmeal and salt into two cups boiling water in saucepan. Stir for one minute. Remove from heat. Add butter and beat well. Add eggs. Beat in milk until well blended.
- Pour into buttered baking disk. Bake in 450 degree oven for 25 minutes. Serve in baking dish.

Prepared for Ricky Van Shelton.

"I think that most performers are so transparent that they don't fool audiences easily."

—RADNEY FOSTER

GRANDPA'S SPOON BREAD

1 lg. carton sour cream
1 stick margarine, melted
1 sm. can cream style corn
1 egg
2 pkgs. corn bread mix

• Preheat oven to 400 degrees. Mix together all ingredients. Pour into greased Pyrex dish. Reduce heat to 350 degrees and bake for 55 to 60 minutes.

Prepared for Grandpa Jones.

"**W**e should be very conscious of making country music shows family events. You see generations of people at live shows. Nashville is a writers' town—as long as those great songs keep coming, we can continue to portray that image."

—BILL CODY

BAKING POWDER BISCUITS

4 cups flour, sifted
5 tsp. Calumet
   Baking Powder
1½ tsp. salt
½–¾ cup shortening
1½ cups milk

- Sift flour once, measure, add baking powder and salt, and sift together into bowl.
- Cut in shortening until mixture looks like coarse meal, using two knives or a wire pastry blender. Add milk as needed, mixing until a soft dough is formed. (The exact amount needed depends upon flour used.)
- Turn dough onto a lightly floured board and knead half a minute to shape. (Takes about 15 turns.) Roll or pat ½ inch thick. Cut with floured 2-inch cutter. Let stand undisturbed for another half-minute for especially well-shaped biscuits.
- Place on ungreased baking sheet. Bake in hot oven at 450 degrees for 12 to 15 minutes.

YIELDS 24 BISCUITS.

Prepared for Garth Brooks.

"A lot of entertainers try to give a lot of messages through their music. I'm not that way."

—NEAL McCOY

DELUXE BUTTERMILK BISCUITS

1 pkg. dry yeast
2 tbsp. warm water
   (105 to 115 degrees)
5 cups all-purpose flour
¼ cup sugar
1 tbsp. baking powder
1 tsp. soda
1 tsp. salt
1 cup shortening
2 cups buttermilk
  melted butter

- Dissolve yeast in warm water, and set aside.
- Combine dry ingredients; cut in shortening with pastry blender until mixture resembles course meal. Add yeast mixture and buttermilk to dry ingredients and mix well.
- Turn dough out on a floured surface and knead lightly 4 or 5 times.
- Roll dough to ½ inch thickness; cut with a 2-inch biscuit cutter.
- Place on greased baking sheets. Brush tops with melted butter. Bake at 400 degrees for 12 to 15 minutes. Freezes well.

YIELDS 3-1/2 DOZEN.

Prepared for Colin Raye.

"**E**very country singer feels that they must be the spokesperson for country music and, in turn, feels the need to get the music out there."

—PAM TILLIS

Part Eight

BEVERAGES

RICH-AND-CREAMY COFFEE PUNCH

1 gal. strong hot coffee
1¼ cups sugar
2 cups whipping cream, whipped
1 pt. vanilla ice cream, softened
1 pt. chocolate ice cream, softened

• Combine coffee and sugar, stirring until sugar dissolves; chill well.
• Fold in whipped cream and ice cream just before serving.

YIELDS ABOUT 5 QUARTS.

Prepared for Leroy Parnell.

"I think that if we do have a definite problem in our business it is that we are trying to develop people who are singers and not entertainers."

—REX ALLEN, JR.

CITRUS PUNCH

2 ozs. citric acid
2 qts. boiling water
5 cups sugar
5 qts. cold water
1 can (46 oz.) pineapple
   juice, chilled
1 can (6 oz.) frozen orange
   juice concentrate,
   thawed and undiluted

- Combine citric acid and boiling water in a ceramic heatproof container; stir until citric acid dissolves. Let mixture stand 24 hours.
- Combine sugar and cold water; stir until sugar is dissolved. Add citric acid mixture, pineapple juice, and orange juice; stir well. Serve over ice.

YIELDS ABOUT 8-1/2 QUARTS.

Prepared for Bryan White.

"**A**n entertainer's career is nothing but peaks and valleys. Some of us survive them and others don't. My peaks and valleys have run pretty concurrent with what's happening in country music."

—REX ALLEN JR.

ORANGE-MINT PUNCH

2 cups sugar
2½ cups water
¼ cup dried mint leaves
1 can (12 oz.) frozen orange juice concentrate, thawed and undiluted
⅓ cup lemon juice
6 cups cold water

- Combine sugar and 2½ cups water in a medium saucepan; bring to a boil, and boil 10 minutes. Stir in mint leaves; steep 1 hour. Strain.
- Stir in remaining ingredients. Serve over crushed ice.

YIELDS ABOUT 2-1/2 QUARTS.

Prepared for Garth Brooks.

"**E**xcitement is great. But you've got to remember where you came from and keep your head—that keeps you personally and musically in order."

—MARK WILLS

BACKSTAGE FRUIT PUNCH

2 cans (46 oz.) pineapple
   juice
2 cans (12 oz.) frozen
   orange juice concen-
   trate, thawed and
   undiluted
1 pkg. (6 oz.) lemon-
   flavored gelatin
4 qts. ginger ale, chilled
   fruit slices (optional)
   maraschino cherries
   (optional)

- Combine first 3 ingredients, stirring well; chill.
- To serve, combine chilled mixture and ginger ale in a punch bowl. Garnish with fruit slices and maraschino cherries, if desired.

YIELDS ABOUT 2 GALLONS.

Prepared for Mark Collie.

"Success is living your dream, not living in a dream world. You can lose sight of the difference when you get caught up in the day to day grind of meeting commitments. Step back and look once in a while."

—DAVE ROBBINS

CLOVES AND MINT LEMONADE

6 lg. lemons
6 whole cloves
5 cups boiling water
2 cups granulated sugar
  juice of two lemons
1 bottle distilled or
    sparkling mineral
    water
  lemon slices
  mint leaves
  ice cubes

- Cut 6 lemons into thin slices. Place in large bowl with cloves; pour in boiling water. Leave 24 hours to marinade. Drain and discard lemon slices and cloves.
- Place marinaded liquid in large pan, add sugar and heat gently until dissolved. Bring to boil and simmer for 10 minutes until liquid is thick and syrupy. Remove from heat; cool.
- Add the fresh lemon juice and pour syrup into a screw-top bottle. Chill.
- To serve, put 1–2 tablespoons syrup into each glass. Fill glass with sparkling water. Garnish with thin lemon slices and mint leaves. Add ice cubes.

Prepared for Pam Tillis.

"Fame is like smoke—it can soon evaporate."
—MINNIE PEARL

Indexes

Photo Index

Quotation Index

Recipe Index